# The Apocalyptic Jesus
## A Debate

D1474178

# The
# Apocalyptic
# Jesus  A Debate

Dale C. Allison

Marcus J. Borg

John Dominic Crossan

Stephen J. Patterson

Robert J. Miller editor

Polebridge
Press

The editor wishes to thank the following for their assistance in reading the draft of this book: John and Mary Dosier, Hershey Julien, Nancy Marshall, and especially Tom Hall, whose numerous suggestions have improved its grammar and style.

*The Apocalyptic Jesus: A Debate*

Published in 2001 by Polebridge Press, P. O. Box 6144, Santa Rosa, California, 95406.

© 2001 by Polebridge Press

ISBN 0-944344-89-5

# Contents

# Contributors

**Dale C. Allison** is Errett M. Grable Professor of New Testament Exegesis and Early Christianity at Pittsburgh Theological Seminary. He has written three books about Jesus, including *Jesus of Nazareth: Millenarian Prophet* (1998). He is also the co-author (with W. D. Davies) of the three-volume *International Critical Commentary* on the Gospel of Matthew (1988–1998).

**Marcus J. Borg** is Hundere Distinguished Professor of Religion and Culture at Oregon State University. He is the author of several best-sellers, including *Meeting Jesus Again for the First Time* (1994) and *The God We Never Knew* (2000).

**John Dominic Crossan** is Professor Emeritus of Biblical Studies, DePaul University, Chicago. Among his many books about Jesus are two land-mark studies: *The Historical Jesus: The Life of a Mediterranean Jewish Peasant* (1991) and *The Birth of Christianity* (1998).

**Robert J. Miller** is Scholar-in-Residence at Westar Institute in Santa Rosa, California. He is the editor of *The Complete Gospels* (rev. ed. 1994) and the author of *The Jesus Seminar and Its Critics* (1999).

**Stephen J. Patterson** is Professor of New Testament at Eden Theological Seminary in St. Louis. He is the author of *The Gospel of Thomas and Jesus* (1993) and *The God of Jesus* (1998).

# Introduction

Robert J. Miller

The name "Jesus" attaches to various data sets. Among other things these data sets include beliefs about personal salvation, narratives about long-ago events, and doctrines about the special status of one particular man. When we say "Jesus" in this book, we mean to designate a particular human being who lived in Palestine during the Roman Era and who died by crucifixion. He was the doer of certain deeds, the thinker of certain thoughts, the sayer of certain words, all of which came to a close at Calvary. This is the human being whom we designate "the historical Jesus."

He poses many puzzles for us. This book focuses on one of them: did the historical Jesus teach that God would put an end to the world as we know it and create a new world of justice and peace? And did Jesus teach that God would do this *soon*, within the lifetime of his own generation? In other words, was the historical Jesus an apocalyptic prophet? This question is the subject of much debate among biblical scholars. Those familiar with current research on the historical Jesus know that scholars disagree on many issues: what Jesus did and did not say and do, the meaning of his teachings and actions, what others thought of him and his message, what he thought about himself, why he was executed, why his movement continued after his death, and so on. However, the question of whether Jesus was an apocalyptic prophet is more than just one question among a long list of others. The way we answer this particular question shapes the way we understand much of the gospel evidence. So the question of whether the historical Jesus was an apocalyptic prophet may well be the single most important one about him because it goes directly to the essential nature of his message and mission. Unfortunately, since

1

biblical scholars are deeply divided on this issue they find themselves in basic disagreement about the fundamental meaning of Jesus' teaching.

## The Problem

All critical scholars agree that the gospels contain both historically reliable material based on memories about Jesus, and historically unreliable material based on his followers' interpretations of his life, death, and teaching. The task of historical criticism is to analyze this complex blend of memory and interpretation in order to distinguish what should be attributed to the historical Jesus and what should be attributed either to progressive elaboration by the rank and file of early Christians who passed on the stories about him, or to the focused creativity of the individual gospel writers.

The death of Jesus by execution is the line of demarcation between what originated with the man Jesus of Nazareth and what originated with various constituents of the communities that looked back to him as their point of reference. The deeds, beliefs, and words that existed before Calvary are called "authentic" or "historical" as a way of placing them on the opposite side of this line from all those beliefs and interpretations that originated later. It is no easy task to sort out the fund of Jesus material that comes down to us. The gospel texts, taken as the whole compositions that they are, certainly belong on *our* side of that line, for they were written no earlier than 40 years after the execution of Jesus. But *some* of the information in the gospels comes from the *other* side of Calvary, from Jesus before he died. The scholarly challenge is to separate the pre-Calvary material from the later elaborations of it. This challenge involves two questions: By what criteria is the sorting to be done? What are the results? In each case, resolving the issue is a work in progress.

Among all the thoughts, words, and deeds that have ever been attributed to Jesus, the present volume focuses on those that cluster around one theme: Jesus' apocalyptic expectation or lack thereof. In this regard, we may begin by observing that the gospels report Jesus making some predictions that are clearly apocalyptic. Here are three examples.

> I swear to you, some of those standing here won't ever taste death before they see God's kingdom set in with power. (Mark 9:1)

I swear to you, this generation certainly won't pass into oblivion before all these things [i.e., the coming of the Son of Man on the clouds, etc.] take place. (Mark 13:30)

I swear to you, you certainly won't make it through the towns of Israel before the Son of Man comes. (Matt 10:23)

Were these predictions spoken by Jesus or were they attributed to him later? Here scholarly opinion divides. While this is the most obvious point of disagreement over whether Jesus was an apocalyptic prophet, there is much more to the debate than different judgments about the authenticity of the predictions about the imminent arrival of the kingdom of God or the day of judgment. There are at least four other important areas of lively dispute.

1. *The "present kingdom" sayings.* In a few gospel passages, Jesus teaches that the kingdom of God is already here. Here are two obvious examples:

You won't be able to observe the coming of God's kingdom. People are not going to be able to say, "Look, here it is!" or "Over there!" On the contrary, God's kingdom is right there in your presence. (Luke 17:20–21)

If by God's finger I drive out demons, then for you the kingdom of God has arrived. (Luke 11:20; Matt 12:28).

Though nearly all scholars regard these sayings as authentic, they differ on their meaning. Some argue that these sayings mean exactly what they say: that the kingdom of God is a present, not a future, reality. For them these sayings are the cornerstone evidence that Jesus was not an apocalypticist. Other scholars maintain that Jesus was an apocalyptic prophet who saw God's imminent kingdom as so near that it was already breaking into his present time. In this view, Jesus announced the beginning of the End.

2. *Ambiguous sayings.* A number of Jesus' sayings can be understood in either an apocalyptic or a non-apocalyptic sense. The beatitudes are prime examples. When Jesus congratulated the poor, the hungry, and the sorrowing (Luke 6:20–21) did he mean that these people enjoyed God's favor right now in their present lives? Or did he congratulate them because their circumstances would soon be reversed when God imposed his rule on earth? The

sayings can legitimately be read either way. The difference in meaning comes not from the sayings themselves but from the larger context one uses to understand them. Another set of examples are Jesus' extraordinary demands to renounce family ties (Luke 14:26; Matt 10:37), to walk away from home and family (Mark 10:29–30), or not to bury one's dead parents (Luke 9:59–60; Matt 8:21–22). Was Jesus challenging people to re-examine all their priorities, even the most sacred ones, in light of the demands of God's present kingdom? Or did Jesus urge this behavior because the social arrangements of the world as we know it will soon be irrelevant in the new world that God will create? Again, both interpretations are tenable. Even some of Jesus' predictions of coming judgment (if they are authentic – and this is by no means agreed on) can be taken in an apocalyptic or a non-apocalyptic sense. When Jesus announces the coming destruction of Jerusalem or when he condemns unrepentant towns (Luke 10:13–15; Matt 11:21–24), is he referring to the imminent Day of Judgment? Or is Jesus speaking in the tradition of prophets like Isaiah and Jeremiah and warning that God will punish Israel with a military disaster?

3. *Ambiguous deeds.* A similar problem of interpretation comes with some of Jesus' deeds. Did he intend his exorcisms to indicate that his battles with evil spirits were the first skirmishes of the imminent final conflict between Good and Evil? Or do his healings show that God's spirit is always and everywhere opposed to all manner of evil and oppression, physical as well as social, economic, and religious? And when Jesus disrupted the money-changing in the temple, was this an enacted symbol of the temple's coming destruction, or was it a protest against its symbolic role as legitimator of the oppressive status quo? Here too, both apocalyptic and non-apocalyptic interpretations are legitimate.

4. *Jesus' place within his religious environment.* Another area of dispute has to do with how we should understand Jesus' relationship to the apocalyptic thinking in first-century Judaism. There were apocalyptic prophets in the first century and some of them attracted a great deal of attention; this means that many people were willing to accept their message that the Day of Judgment was at hand. One of these prophets was John the Baptizer. Since Jesus was baptized by John it seems certain that, at least for a while, he shared John's apocalyptic outlook. However, some of Jesus' teachings about the kingdom of God, especially in

his parables, seem to call into question some basic assumptions of apocalypticism. Uncertainty about how to interpret these teachings makes it debatable whether Jesus remained apocalyptic throughout his ministry or whether he came to believe that God was already king, but not the kind of king who imposed his rule through the fiery judgment described by John.

While other problems in interpreting the gospels are relevant to the issue of whether the historical Jesus was an apocalyptic prophet, the problems sketched above are the most important in the current scholarly debate and show why the problem is so complex.

## Defining Terms

At this point, we need to clarify our terminology by defining two key terms: *eschatology* and *apocalypticism*. These words can cause confusion because different writers use them in different ways, sometimes without defining them. Since this book is an exchange among scholars with different positions, it is crucial to make sure everyone agrees on the meanings of key terms lest disagreements about the historical Jesus result from misunderstanding one another's terminology.

The term *eschatology* comes from the Greek word *eschaton*, which means "end." In a general sense eschatology is a set of beliefs about the end of the world. In biblical studies it refers to a way of thinking that is centered on the end of history. For Jews and Christians this end is understood to be a culmination, not a cessation: the end of history is the fulfillment of God's plan for humanity. Both Judaism and Christianity exhibit a variety of eschatologies. Some of them envision the literal end of the world, in the sense of the destruction of the material universe. Some of them envision not the end of the physical earth, but rather the end of the world as we know it, that is, the end of all the established orders that create injustice and misery. Some eschatologies envision God transforming the natural world so that it becomes miraculously abundant and free of disease and natural disasters. Some eschatologies are more specifically focused on the social, political, and religious transformations that will ensure that people live according to God's will. Despite these variations in Jewish and Christian eschatological hopes, all biblical eschatologies are united by the fundamental conviction that God will prevail in the

end. In terms of the specific concern of this book, to say that the
message and mission of the historical Jesus was eschatological, is
to say that it was focused on the culmination of history and the
fulfillment of God's plan for humanity.

*Apocalypticism* is one kind of eschatology. Thus, all apocalypticism is eschatological, but not every eschatology is apocalyptic.
Apocalypticism is a complex phenomenon that appears in a variety of expressions. In this book apocalypticism is understood as a
kind of eschatology that envisions the end of history coming soon
and brought about by an overpowering divine intervention. This
occurrence will be evident to all people and will be preceded by
cataclysmic events. Thus to describe Jesus as an apocalyptic
prophet is to claim that he taught that in the very near future,
within the lifetime of his contemporaries, God was going to intervene directly and decisively to bring history to its divinely
planned fulfillment.

## A History of the Question

The question of the relationship of Jesus to apocalypticism is not
a new one in biblical studies. It has been a central aspect of the
study of the historical Jesus for over a century. In the nineteenth
century numerous European books about Jesus told the story of
his life and explained his teachings outside the interpretive framework of Christian orthodoxy. Eschewing belief in Jesus' divinity,
these "Lives of Jesus" portrayed him as a teacher of enlightened
morality and eternal spiritual truths. In 1906, Albert Schweitzer
published *The Quest of the Historical Jesus,* a book that became
a milestone in biblical scholarship. Schweitzer analyzed dozens of
Lives of Jesus and drew a conclusion that has haunted New
Testament scholars ever since: the authors of these books invari-
ably portrayed Jesus as the embodiment of their own ideals.
Although these books broke away from the christological doctrines of the Church, they were far from being objective historical
accounts. Consciously or not, these nineteenth-century authors
used their own moral and spiritual ideals as the interpretive framework within which they crafted their portraits of Jesus from the
gospel material. Their different Jesuses looked much like their own
best selves. As Schweitzer diagnosed the situation, the fundamen-

tal error common to all these authors was that they were unaware of, or unconcerned with, the problem of historical distance.

Jesus belonged to a world very different from our own, not only in time, place, culture, and language, but different also in the basic ways in which people thought about God, the world, and human nature. The Lives of Jesus that Schweitzer reviewed failed to appreciate that Jesus was a figure from the distant past with a message suited to his own particular place in history. Instead they assumed that their own highest ideals were also his. In short, they treated Jesus as if he would be at home in the nineteenth century.

Schweitzer pointed to one scholar who had avoided this trap, Johannes Weiss. According to Schweitzer, Weiss was the first to correctly understand the nature of Jesus' message about the kingdom of God. Weiss achieved this by insisting that "all modern ideas, even in their subtlest form, must be eliminated from it [the kingdom of God]." For Schweitzer, Weiss's work "seems to break a spell. It closes one epoch and begins another."[1]

Weiss had published *Jesus' Proclamation of the Kingdom of God* in 1892, nine years before Schweitzer's work on Jesus. Weiss was the first scholar to develop a critical portrait of Jesus as an apocalyptic prophet. Weiss's primary purpose was to respond to a widespread understanding of his time that for Jesus the kingdom of God was an ethical ideal. In this view Jesus revealed universal and eternally valid moral teachings that represented the ultimate stage of humanity's moral development. A prominent theologian of the day, Albrecht Ritschl (Weiss's father-in-law), put it this way: "The kingdom of God is the divinely ordained highest good of the community founded through God's revelation in Christ."[2] According to Ritschl, Jesus not only taught about the kingdom; he made it a reality through his example of a life of complete obedience to God.

Weiss rejected both the understanding of the kingdom as a spiritual reality that can be actualized by moral behavior, and the notion of Jesus as a founder of the kingdom. What Weiss found in the gospels was a Jesus who announced and prepared people for the coming of a kingdom that was entirely the work of God, a kingdom that had political as well as religious dimensions.

---

1. Schweitzer, *Quest*, 239.
2. Ritschl, "Instruction;" quoted from Dawes, *Quest*, 222.

According to Weiss, Jesus believed that the world was not receptive to the coming of God's kingdom because it was under the sway of another kingdom, that of Satan. Jesus had some profound experience at the start of his ministry that convinced him that he had overcome Satan. Although we do not know how Jesus came to this conviction (perhaps in a vision, or perhaps in his temptation in the desert), he saw his work of healing and exorcism as a struggle against the kingdom of Satan, whose power had been broken and whose agents, the demons, could not resist Jesus or those who used his name. The kingdom of God would come in the destruction of Satan's kingdom, but would also involve the release of Israel from political oppression, although this political aspect was secondary to Jesus' main concern for "what was genuinely religious in the kingdom of God and ethical preparation for its coming."[3]

Jesus' role was not to establish the kingdom, said Weiss. That was up to God alone. Jesus was to prepare the way for the kingdom through his battle with Satan and through his moral teaching. "He is the sower who scatters the seed of the Word in men's hearts."[4] Jesus originally thought that God would bring the kingdom during his lifetime. Eventually, however, he came to believe that he must die in order for the kingdom to come. Before the kingdom could come the guilt of God's people had to be removed, and in this light Jesus regarded his own death as a necessary "ransom." Jesus believed that he was to be the Messiah, but only after his death. God would exalt him and later send him back to earth in glory as the heavenly Son of Man. When God thus finally establishes his kingdom, he will transfer the power of judgment to the exalted Jesus. He and his faithful followers "will rule over this newborn people of the twelve tribes, which will include even the Gentiles."[5]

Weiss's work was a major influence on Schweitzer's understanding of the historical Jesus, which Schweitzer presented in *The Mystery of the Kingdom of God* in 1901. As discussed above, Schweitzer's study of nineteenth-century Jesus books convinced him that their basic error was in treating Jesus as a contemporary, as if he would be at home with modern ideas. In his own work, therefore, Schweitzer emphasized that Jesus is a stranger to the

---

3. Weiss, *Jesus' Proclamation*; quoted from Dawes, *Quest*, 178.
4. Weiss, *Jesus' Proclamation*; quoted from Dawes, *Quest*, 173.
5. Weiss, *Jesus' Proclamation*; quoted from Dawes, *Quest*, 180.

modern world. In no place is this clearer than in the central element of Jesus' outlook: its eschatological orientation. Schweitzer coined the term "thoroughgoing eschatology" to characterize the essence of Jesus' teaching and mission. (By "eschatology" Schweitzer meant what we have defined as apocalypticism.)

For Schweitzer, a key verse for understanding Jesus is Matt 10:23: "I swear to you, you certainly won't make it through the towns of Israel before the Son of Man comes." This verse is part of the discourse in which Jesus commissions the twelve to preach and heal in the villages (Matt 10:5–33). Schweitzer draws our attention to three aspects of this mission. First, Jesus does not instruct the disciples to pass on his teachings, but rather to issue an urgent warning to repent. Second, Jesus saw this mission as the last one. Matt 10:23 shows that he expected the End to come before it was finished. Third, Jesus warns the disciples to expect persecution, which Schweitzer takes to be part of the tribulations that come in the Last Days as the powers of evil stage their final revolt against the inevitable victory of God.

When the disciples returned from this mission and reported their success, Schweitzer argued, Jesus believed that his work was done. He had prepared the way of the Lord and all was now ready for the coming of the kingdom. When nothing happened, Jesus had to rethink his expectations. Jesus had believed himself to be the Messiah since his baptism, although he had kept this belief to himself. After the mission of the twelve to Israel, Jesus came to a different understanding of his messianic calling. Reflecting on the death of John the Baptizer and on the Suffering Servant passages from Isaiah, Jesus came to believe that God was laying upon him the punishment due for Israel's sin. He would endure a death like John's: he would be executed as a public criminal by the political authorities. His death would atone for the people's guilt, and so the End could come without a general tribulation. Jesus embraced this destiny, expecting that he would die on the literal Last Day. His "journey to Jerusalem was the funeral march to victory."[6] Even on the cross Jesus was expectant, refusing the offer of a drug to dull his pain so as to remain alert.

Schweitzer succeeded in his purpose of portraying Jesus as a stranger to the modern world. Indeed, Schweitzer's Jesus was so alien to modern sensibilities that most Christians were appalled

6. Schweitzer, *Mystery of the Kingdom*; quoted in Dawes, *Quest*, 200.

by him. However, critical biblical scholars absorbed a powerful lesson from Weiss and Schweitzer: if you understand the apocalypticism in the gospels to come from the historical Jesus you have resisted the natural tendency to fashion Jesus in your own image. The lesson stuck. Although historical Jesus scholarship in the twentieth century went through distinct phases and shows a healthy variety of methods and results, through it all ran a broad consensus that Jesus expected an imminent End and that he looked to the future for the establishment of the kingdom of God. This consensus was not unanimous, however. Several respected scholars questioned it on the basis of studies of the parables and the Son of Man sayings. The discovery of the lost Gospel of Thomas in the middle of the century introduced important new evidence that for some has further eroded the earlier consensus. And important research on Q in the eighties was likewise taken by some scholars to weigh against an apocalyptic Jesus. Nevertheless, that the historical Jesus was an apocalyptic prophet stood as a secure majority opinion of the twentieth century until the 1990s.

The last decade of the century saw this consensus challenged as never before. In 1993 the Jesus Seminar, a group of over seventy scholars, published the results of its six-year collaborative project of evaluating the historical value of the sayings of Jesus. The Seminar concluded that the historical Jesus was not an apocalyptic prophet. Three members of the Seminar published independent research on Jesus that arrived at the same conclusion. The most extensive, the most influential, and the most contested of these studies is *The Historical Jesus: The Life of a Mediterranean Jewish Peasant* (1991) by John Dominic Crossan (condensed in *Jesus: A Revolutionary Biography*, 1994). Marcus Borg, who had already challenged the apocalyptic consensus in an article in 1986 and in a popular book on the historical Jesus in 1987 (*Jesus: A New Vision*), explored the implications of a non-apocalyptic understanding of Jesus for Christian belief and spirituality in *Meeting Jesus Again for the First Time* (1994). Stephen Patterson argued against an apocalyptic Jesus in a 1995 article and in *The God of Jesus* (1998). The work of the Jesus Seminar and of Crossan, Borg, and Patterson has been criticized on several fronts, but the primary item of disagreement usually seems to be the apocalyptic Jesus. Many scholars apparently find it unthinkable that Jesus was not an apocalyptic prophet. Virtually every scholar who went on record against the work of the Jesus Seminar or

Crossan or Borg repeated Schweitzer's accusation that these scholars were modernizing Jesus and remaking him in their own image. Unfortunately, much of this criticism either devolved into caricatures and personal attacks or merely reiterated the modern consensus position as if it were self-evident that Jesus simply had to be an apocalyptic prophet.[7]

In 1998 Dale Allison published *Jesus of Nazareth, Millenarian Prophet*, a fresh and learned portrait of the historical Jesus as an End Time prophet. ("Millenarianism" refers to the social expression of apocalyptic convictions. Apocalypticism is a set of beliefs; groups formed on the basis of these beliefs are "millenarian.") Several features of Allison's book mark it as the most important recent presentation of this position. Allison goes beyond repeating the standard arguments and develops a new, multi-faceted method for conducting historical Jesus research. Especially important is his use of cross-cultural studies of millenarianism to compare Jesus and his followers to a wide range of apocalyptic leaders and movements from other historical and cultural contexts. This enables Allison to see, for example, new significance in Jesus' teachings on wealth and sex. Allison's book is also important for the way he engages scholarly work with which he disagrees. He criticizes the work of Crossan, Borg, and Patterson in a fair and responsible manner. He represents their positions accurately, grapples with their specific arguments, and refrains from polemics. This is how scholarly criticism should proceed, though Allison's high standards unfortunately seem to be the exception rather than the rule. Allison conducts his critique in a way that opens the door for further conversations that carry the potential for increasing everyone's understanding.

## The Plan of This Book

This book is an extended exchange between Allison on the one hand and Borg, Crossan, and Patterson on the other. The book aims to facilitate this exchange in such a way that the participants go beyond simply staking out and defending opposing positions. In this book they have the opportunity to respond to one another, to assess the debate, to engage in self-criticism, and to explore the broader implications of each position. The book has three parts.

7. For an analysis of and response to this and other criticisms of the Jesus Seminar, see Miller, *Jesus Seminar*, especially chapter 4.

*Part One: The Debate* (chapters 1–3). This longest part of the book is structured as a formal academic debate. In chapter 1 Allison summarizes the argument in his recent book, explaining his case for an apocalyptic Jesus. In chapter 2 Borg, Crossan, and Patterson present their cases for a non-apocalyptic Jesus, criticize Allison's argument, and respond to the criticisms Allison made in his book of their published positions. In chapter 3 Allison comes back to grapple with the criticisms and arguments in chapter 2.

*Part Two: Taking Stock* (chapter 4). This brief but important part of the book is what makes it a genuine dialogue rather than simply another academic debate. In chapter 4 each participant looks back at the exchange in Part One and assesses the strengths and weaknesses of each position by answering two pairs of questions: What is the strongest point in my position and the weakest point in the other position? Conversely, what is the strongest point in the other position and the weakest point in mine? The first two questions call for evaluations that are routine in debates, i.e., summations of why one's position is better than its opposite. The last two questions call on our participants to acknowledge the strength of the position they disagree with and the weakness of their own. Although the intellectual benefits of self-criticism are obvious, it is exceptionally rare for scholars to engage in it publicly. Our participants have agreed to it in good faith because they want to make this book as much a dialogue as a debate. To be sure, the debate is vigorous and sincere, as is clear from Part One. But a debate has a limited objective: winning an argument. The aim of a dialogue, on the other hand, is for those who disagree to work together to seek whatever truth is available to them. In debate one seeks to refute an opponent's position, whereas in a dialogue there is the freedom to acknowledge that both sides have strengths and weaknesses. In a debate we try to convince others; in a dialogue we try to learn from those with whom we disagree.

*Part Three: So What?* (chapters 5–6). Here we explore what is at stake in the discussion. As interesting and important as the debate over Jesus is in itself, reconstructions of the historical Jesus inevitably shape our understanding both of the development of early Christianity and the theological dimensions of contemporary Christian life. Accordingly, our participants reflect on what difference it makes whether Jesus was or was not apocalyptic, both on our historical understanding of first-century Christianity and on what it means to be a follower of Jesus today. In chapter 5 the scholars explain how their understanding of the historical Jesus helps us make better sense out of what we know about the early Christians. In chapter 6 the participants offer their reflections on the implications of both positions for Christian belief and practice today.

# Part 1:
# The Debate

# Jesus was an Apocalyptic Prophet

Dale Allison

> See the value of imagination . . . . We imagined what might have hap-
> pened, acted upon the supposition, and find ourselves justified.
>
> – Sherlock Holmes

Historians of the Jesus tradition are story-tellers, not scientists. We can do no more than aspire to fashion a narrative that is more persuasive than competing narratives, one that satisfies our aesthetical and historical sensibilities because of its apparent ability to clarify more data in a more satisfactory fashion than its rivals.

How is this done? Our first move is not to discover which sayings or what complexes might be authentic. Rather, we should be looking for an explanatory model or matrix by which to order as much of the data as possible. The initial task is to create a context, a primary frame of reference, for the Jesus tradition, a context which may assist us in determining both the authenticity of traditions and their interpretation. One suspects that most of us have probably been doing something like this all along even when pretending to be getting our results by passing them through our so-called criteria of authenticity. We do not come to our task with nothing more than the Jesus tradition, a knowledge of first-century history, and our criteria in hand. We also always bring with us a story, formed or half-formed, a story about Jesus, a story made up of expectations and presuppositions that tacitly guide us in our use of our clumsy criteria. This is one reason we have such a variety of results from various scholars.

It would seem to follow that we should initially be concerned less with refining our criteria of authenticity than with worrying about how to establish a story that can usefully arrange our mass of data into some coherent patterns. If we do not and cannot

17

come to our data with a *tabula rasa*, we might as well examine the slate. Here I agree with Dom, who has written:

> Nobody initiates historical Jesus research without any idea about Jesus. It is therefore a little ingenuous to start from certain texts and act as if one discovered the historical Jesus at the other end of one's analysis. There is and should be always an initial hypothesis that one tests against the data.[1]

But what should be our "initial hypothesis" that we "test against the data"? Modern scholarship offers us a christological buffet. We can, as I do, interpret the tradition on the supposition that Jesus was an apocalyptic prophet much like the Baptist. Or we can make sense of it by maintaining that he was a Zealot and revolutionary. The Jesus tradition can also be analyzed according to the notion that Jesus was first of all a magician, or first of all a Pharisee, or first of all a Jewish peasant Cynic, or first of all a healer and exorcist. It is possible to construe the data – to interpret on the one hand and to discard on the other – in accord with each explanatory model. Reasonable, well-meaning people have done so.

This should not surprise, for one can always construct competing hypotheses for the very same set of data, just as one can draw any number of curves through a finite set of points to create a thousand different pictures. Recall the two very different stories told to explain the evidence at the O.J. Simpson murder trials. One account held that all the evidence pointed to Simpson because he was guilty. The other claimed that all the evidence pointed to him because the police set him up. It is always possible to explain one set of facts with more than one story. So how do we choose which story to believe?

Philosophers of science have much discussed the nature of competing paradigms or explanatory models in science and how shifts of vision occur – how, for instance, the Aristotelian theory of motion gave way to Galileo's theory of motion. What changes during most scientific revolutions is not the extant data but their interpretive context.

To what extent this is a rational enterprise, and to what extent our models actually correspond to reality, are involved philosophical questions beyond the scope of this chapter. I must be content

---

1. Crossan, "Materials and Methods," 10.

with remarking that, even if some philosophers are now conceptual relativists and in general deny that any one theory can claim exclusively to be the right way of looking at something, most New Testament scholars still share a universe of discourse, and within that discourse it makes sense to ask whether one paradigm or interpretive norm is better than some other (just as it makes sense to ask which story about O. J. Simpson is the most plausible). Not all of our pertinent facts are "theory-laden" in a debilitating sense, nor do most New Testament scholars live in truly different conceptual worlds. It is reasonable to hope that sometimes one party in a dispute can in fact offer better reasons for its conclusions than another party.

For the last hundred years many New Testament scholars have, as outlined in Bob's introduction to this volume, approached the sayings of Jesus with the paradigm of Jesus as apocalyptic prophet. The works of Johannes Weiss and Albert Schweitzer brought us that paradigm. Many scholars underwent a sort of conversion experience (one which is still replayed today when someone brought up in church with a non-apocalyptic understanding of the kingdom of God goes off to college or graduate school and learns to think otherwise). Despite both initial and continued resistance, more and more scholars came to see that the story of Jesus as apocalyptic prophet offered the best research program. Its simplicity, scope, explanatory power, and parallels in the history of religion commended it.

The basic apocalyptic paradigm has been in place now for a century. It has become an academic tradition that has enabled its social constituency to order its reading of New Testament texts; and its proponents remain many. But some now think that, although it has lived a useful life, the old paradigm now needs to be retired. Few deny that the apocalyptic interpretation of Jesus has brought us much illumination, for it has revealed once and for all that many sayings contain an apocalyptic eschatology. But my fellow contributors to this volume believe that many of those sayings are secondary and that their addition greatly distorted things. So these scholars are offering us a new paradigm: Jesus as aphoristic sage (Marcus) or as Jewish peasant Cynic (Dom).

It has been said that science progresses one funeral at a time, that a new theory does not always triumph by convincing its opponents but because the opponents die and a new generation, uncommitted to the past, comes along. Although I think it an unlikely eventuality, I can imagine the new, non-apocalyptic paradigm establishing itself as the new orthodoxy when those of us who grew up on Schweitzer have died out. It is my conviction, however, that, if the old paradigm is ever discarded, a grave error will have been made. The proposition that Jesus was an eschatological prophet with what one may call an apocalyptic scenario should remain the matrix within which to establish and interpret the authentic traditions.

## The Best Research Program

We cannot confirm the new paradigm or refute the old one by sharpening the traditional criteria of authenticity any more than by doing exegesis or creating tradition-histories, which are so speculative. For how we perform these tasks always depends upon the assumptions we bring to them. So, to repeat, a paradigm should, if possible, be settled upon prior to and independently of our evaluation of the historicity of individual items in the Jesus tradition. Our goal is not to be free of prejudices but to have the right prejudices. Can this be done?

I believe that we can indeed adopt the right prejudices and say a good deal about Jesus apart from detailed evaluation of the origin of various complexes. Moreover, when we undertake this endeavor we are back with the conventional paradigm of Jesus as apocalyptic prophet. Here are the reasons for thinking this:

1. Passages from a wide variety of sources show us that many early followers of Jesus thought the eschatological climax to be near. Consider the following, from six different first-century Christian writers:

> **Acts 3:19–21** "Repent, therefore, and turn to God so that times of refreshing may come from the presence of the Lord, and that he may send the Messiah appointed for you, that is, Jesus, who must remain in heaven until the time of universal restoration that God announced long ago through his holy prophets."
>
> **Rom 13:11** "Besides this, you know what time it is, how it is now the moment for you to wake from sleep. For salvation is nearer to us now than when we became believers."
>
> **1 Cor 16:22** "Our Lord, come!" (a traditional formulation; see Rev 22:20)
>
> **Heb 10:37** "In a very little while, the one who is coming will come and will not delay."

**James 5:8** "You must also be patient. Strengthen your hearts, for the coming of the Lord is near."

**1 Pet 4:17** "For the time has come for judgment to begin with the household of God."

**Rev 22:20** "The one who testifies to these things says, 'Surely I am coming soon.'"

We also know that, in the pre-Easter period, Jesus himself was closely associated with John the Baptist, whose public speech, if the synoptics are any guide at all, featured frequent allusion to the eschatological judgment, conceived as imminent (see Luke 3:7–17, which preserves material from the Q source). Jesus indeed was baptized by John. Obviously then, there must have been significant ideological continuity between the two men. So, as many have observed again and again, to reconstruct a Jesus who did not have a strong eschatological or apocalyptic orientation entails discontinuity not only between him and people who took themselves to be furthering his cause, but also between him and the Baptist — that is, discontinuity with the movement out of which he came as well as with the movement that came out of him. Isn't presumption against this?

2. The canonical Gospels, traditions in Acts, and the letters of Paul are united in relating that at least several pre-Easter followers of Jesus, soon after his crucifixion, declared that "God raised Jesus from the dead" (see Mark 16:6; Acts 2:24; Rom 10:9; 1 Thes 1:10) or vindicated him by "the resurrection of the dead ones" (Acts 4:2; see Rom 1:4). The fact of their combined testimony on this matter is not doubted by anyone, so we may ask why people made this claim, why they affirmed the occurrence of an eschatological event. The best explanation is that several influential individuals came to their post-Easter experiences, whatever they were, with certain categories and expectations antecedently fixed: that they already, because of Jesus' teaching, envisaged the general resurrection to be imminent. This is why "resurrection" was for many the chief category by which to interpret Jesus' vindication.

3. According to Mark 15:33, when Jesus died there was a strange darkness (see Amos 8:9–10). According to Matt 27:51–53, there was also a strong earthquake (see Zech 14:5) and a resurrection of the dead (see Ezekiel 37 and Zech 14:4–5). According to John's Gospel, Jesus' death was "the judgment of the world" (John 12:31) and brought down the reign of Satan (John 16:11). According to Paul, Jesus is "the first fruits of those who have died"

(1 Cor 15:20) – a metaphor which assumes that the eschatological harvest is underway, that the resurrection of Jesus is only the beginning of the general resurrection of the dead. Given its multiple attestation in Paul, the synoptics, and John, the habit of associating the end of Jesus with eschatological motifs must go back to very early times.

What explains this habit? The best answer is that, while Jesus was yet with them, his followers – as Luke 19:11 plainly tells us – "supposed that the kingdom of God was to appear immediately" (see Acts 1:6). They foresaw apocalyptic suffering followed by eschatological vindication, tribulation followed by resurrection. So when Jesus was, in the event, crucified and seen alive again, his followers, instead of abandoning their apocalyptic hopes, did what one would expect them to do: they sought to correlate expectations with circumstances. This is why they believed that in Jesus' end the eschaton had begun to unfold, and why early Christian texts associate the death and resurrection of Jesus with what appear to be eschatological events.

4. The Roman world of the first century was, in the words of Helmut Koester, "dominated by prophetic eschatology," and the apocalyptic writings of Judaism, which share "the general eschatological spirit" of the Roman imperial period,[2] put us in touch with a type of eschatology that was well known in Jesus' time and place. Not only did the sacred collection itself contain apocalyptic materials – for example, Isaiah 24–27, Daniel, Zechariah 9–14 – but also portions of 1 Enoch, some of the Jewish Sibylline Oracles, and the Testament of Moses were in circulation in Jesus' day; and the decades after Jesus saw the appearance of 4 Ezra, 2 Baruch, and the Apocalypse of Abraham. His time was also when the Dead Sea Scrolls, so many of which are charged with apocalyptic expectation, were presumably being composed or copied and studied. The point, reinforced by Josephus' remarks on the general popularity of the apocalyptic book of Daniel,[3] is simply that the sort of eschatology Schweitzer attributed to Jesus was indeed flourishing in Jesus' day. Social and political circumstances were, as Dom has made clear in his big book on Jesus, probably ripe for the production of a millenarian movement; and the sense of an imminent transformation appears to have been shared by many.

2. Koester, "Jesus," 10–11.
3. *Antiquities* 10.268.

We can make the inference from the New Testament itself. For in the words of Barnabas Lindars,

> the rapid expansion of Christianity would really be inexplicable except against the background of a widespread feeling amongst Jews of the day that they were living in the End Time. For it is . . . only because of the pre-understanding of the Bible in this eschatological sense, attested not only in Qumran and apocalyptic, but also to some extent in rabbinic sources, that the church's application of the whole range of Old Testament to Jesus could be felt to be a plausible undertaking and find acceptance.[4]

The point for us is this: to propose that Jesus thought the end to be near is just to say that he believed what many others in his time and place believed.

5. Several New Testament texts compare Jesus with some of his contemporaries. In Luke 7:33–34 (from Q) Jesus compares his own ministry with the ministry of John the Baptist. In Mark 6:14 Herod Antipas says that Jesus is John the Baptist risen from the dead. Mark 8:28 reports that "people" thought Jesus to be like John the Baptist. And according to Acts 5:35–39, Rabbi Gamaliel compared Jesus and his followers with Theudas and his movement as well as with Judas the Galilean and his movement. Now John the Baptist, Theudas, and Judas the Galilean were moved by eschatological expectation or hope for Jewish restoration. John proclaimed a near end[5] and was thought of as a prophet. Theudas claimed to be a prophet, acted as a new Moses, and was viewed as a threat by the Romans. Judas the Galilean,[6] sought independence for the Jewish people with the help of God. What follows? The comparisons in the canonical gospels and Acts, most of which are attributed to outsiders and which would be unlikely to have been generated by insiders, would be natural if Jesus was remembered as an apocalyptic prophet who proclaimed that God's kingdom would replace the Roman kingdom. They are not easily explained if he was not so remembered.

The five arguments just introduced are straightforward and powerful. They involve no special pleading nor any questionable argumentation. They are, moreover, mutually reinforcing. That

---

4. Lindars, "The Place of the Old Testament," 62.
5. Even Origen, *Homily on Luke* 23, recognized that John's words in Luke 3 most naturally refer to "the end of time."
6. See Josephus, *Antiquities* 18.5.

Jesus was baptized by an eschatological prophet and had among his followers people who proclaimed a near end, that certain followers of Jesus proclaimed his resurrection soon after the crucifixion, that his passion and vindication were associated with eschatological motifs, that many first-century Jews expected an apocalyptic scenario to unfold in their near future, and that our sources compare Jesus with others who believed in such a scenario or at least expected God soon to rule Palestine – these indisputable facts together tell us that Jesus held hopes close to those attributed to him by Weiss and Schweitzer. The evidence is, to be sure, circumstantial, but then one recalls what Thoreau famously said: "Some circumstantial evidence is very strong, as when you find a trout in the milk."

## Apocalyptic Sayings of Jesus

The conclusion that Jesus was an eschatological prophet establishes itself, let me emphasize, apart from detailed evaluation of the Jesus tradition. But the sayings only confirm what we can infer on other grounds. For in our sources Jesus speaks of the consummation as temporally near:

**Luke 10:9 (from Q)** "The kingdom of God has come near to you."

**Mark 9:1** "Truly I tell you, there are some standing here who will not taste death until they see that the kingdom of God has come with power."

**Mark 13:30** "Truly I tell you, this generation will not pass away until all these things have taken place."

**Matt 10:23** "Truly I tell you, you will not have gone through all the towns of Israel before the Son of Man comes."

**Thom 111:1** "The heavens and the earth will roll up in your presence."

There are additional texts, moreover, that have Jesus pronouncing eschatological judgment upon contemporaries and otherwise announcing or presupposing that the final fulfillment of God's judgment and saving work are nigh. Here are just a few:

**Luke 11:49–51 (from Q)** "Therefore also the Wisdom of God said, 'I will send them prophets and apostles, some of whom they will kill and persecute,' so that this generation may be charged with all the blood of all the prophets shed since the foundation of the world, from the blood of Abel to the blood of Zechariah, who perished between the altar and the sanctuary. Yes, I tell you, it will be charged against this generation."

**Luke 12:40 (from Q)** "You must be ready, for the Son of Man is coming at an unexpected hour."

**Luke 17:26–27 (from Q)** "Just as it was in the days of Noah, so too it will be in the days of the Son of Man. They were eating and drinking, and marrying and being given in marriage, until the day Noah entered the ark, and the flood came and destroyed all of them."

**Mark 1:15** "The time is fulfilled, and the kingdom of God has come near; repent and believe in the good news."

**Mark 13:28–29** "From the fig tree learn its lesson: as soon as its branch becomes tender and puts forth its leaves, you know that summer is near. So also, when you see these things taking place, you know that he is near, at the very gates."

**Luke 18:7–8** "And will not God grant justice to his chosen ones who cry to him day and night? Will he delay long in helping them? I tell you, he will quickly grant justice to them."

**Luke 21:34–36** "Be on guard so that your hearts are not weighed down with dissipation and drunkenness and the worries of this life, and that day does not catch you unexpectedly, like a trap. For it will come upon all who live on the face of the whole earth. Be alert at all times, praying that you may have the strength to escape all these things that will take place, and to stand before the Son of Man."

**Matt 25:13** "Keep awake therefore, for you know neither the day nor the hour."

How came all this matter into the Jesus tradition? Does not the agreement between the sayings tradition and what we otherwise know of Jesus constitute an initial reason for hope that the sayings tradition preserves some authentic material?

Some might wish to complain that just setting verses before the reader is illegitimate. Don't we have to look at each unit one by one, submit them all to detailed historical-critical analysis, and only then use them as evidence for this or that? My answer is No, for the following reason. When we look back upon our encounters with others, our most vivid and reliable memories are often not precise but general. I may, for instance, not remember exactly what you said to me last year, but I may recall approximately what you said, or retain a general impression, the gist. It is like vaguely recollecting the approximate shape, size, and contents of a room one was in many years ago – a room which has, in the mind's eye, lost all color and detail. After our short-term memories have become long-term memories they suffer progressive abbreviation. I am not sure I remember a single sentence that either of my beloved grandparents on my father's side ever said to me. But I nonetheless know and cherish the *sorts* of things that they said to me.

All of this matters for study of the Jesus tradition because it goes against universal human experience to suppose that early Christians, let us say, accurately recorded many of Jesus' words but somehow came away with false general impressions of him. If the tradents of the Jesus tradition got the big picture or the larger patterns wrong, then they almost certainly also got the details – that is, the sentences – wrong. It is precarious to urge that we can find the truth about Jesus on the basis of a few dozen sayings deemed to be authentic if those sayings are interpreted contrary to the general impressions conveyed by the early tradition in its entirety. If Jesus was, for example, either a violent revolutionary or a secular sage (neither of which is proposed by any contributor to this book), then the tradition about him, which offers a pacifistic and religious sage, is so misleading that we cannot much use it for investigation of the pre-Easter period – and so we cannot know that Jesus was either a violent revolutionary or a secular sage. Here skepticism devours itself. The conclusion refutes the premises.

## Memories of Jesus

The first-century Jesus tradition is, to state the obvious, not a collection of totally disparate and wholly unrelated materials. As everyone knows, certain themes and motifs and rhetorical strategies are consistently attested over a wide range of material. The point is that it is in these themes and motifs and rhetorical strategies, if it is anywhere, that we are likely to have an accurate memory. Indeed, several of these themes and motifs and strategies are sufficiently well attested that we have a choice to make. Either they tend to preserve pre-Easter memories or they do not. In the former case we may know enough to begin to authenticate individual items: the general will help us with the particular. But in the latter case our questing for Jesus is not just interminable but probably pointless and we should consider surrendering to ignorance. If the tradition is so misleading in its broad features, then we can hardly make much of its details.

Any objective inventory of the major themes and motifs that appear again and again in the Jesus tradition would surely include the following:

- The kingdom of God
- Future reward

- Future judgment
- Suffering/persecution for the saints
- Victory over evil powers
- A sense that something new is here or at hand
- The importance of John the Baptist

The regular reappearance of these seven items readily invites an eschatological interpretation of Jesus. When put together they foretell a utopia known as "the kingdom (of God)" that is already manifesting itself notwithstanding great opposition. We have here the standard pattern of Jewish messianism, which is also found in millennial movements world-wide — a time of tribulation followed by a time of unprecedented blessedness. To this extent, then, the Jesus tradition is in line with my earlier conclusion that Jesus was an eschatological prophet who expected God's rule to come shortly.

No one can dispute that the themes and motifs and strategies just listed are widely attested in the Jesus tradition. The relevant question is what we should make of this fact. My own conviction is that, for reasons given above, we should probably either posit that these themes and motifs go back to Jesus or reject them in their entirety. This is of course not a statement about the authenticity of any particular text cited on the previous pages. Here it is the collective weight of the evidence, the pattern created by the multitude, that is being considered; the accuracy of any particular unit is another matter.

Sometimes, as with what engineers call a statically determinate structure, everything stands or falls together. It can be all or nothing. In the present instance, either the tradition instructs us that Jesus spoke often about the kingdom of God, future reward, future judgment and so on, or the tradition is not a useful source for Jesus and we should start questing for someone else. It is my working hypothesis that the former is the case.

Although my working hypothesis is not groundless, it is not the result of an irrefutable argument, nor can it be vindicated by a few observations. It is not a verdict reached by self-evident steps from self-evident truths and clear observations. It is, rather, informed guesswork, a postulate with which to work. This means that its evidence is seen in its consequences. That is, its claim to truth lies in its explanatory power as time goes on and it is applied to ever enlarging arrays of texts and observations. If we can tell good stories with this working hypothesis, then well and good.

But if we could not tell such good stories, or if we could tell better stories with some other working hypothesis, then we would have to reconsider.

I conclude this chapter with two observations that bolster my understanding of Jesus. First, that Jesus composed sayings with the sort of eschatology I attribute to him appears true not only because some of those sayings illuminate or are illuminated by the paradigm of Jesus as eschatological prophet, but also because they satisfy other indices. Consider, for instance, the paraphrase of Mic 7:6 preserved in Matt 10:34–36 ("Do not think that I have come to bring peace to the earth; I have not come to bring peace, but a sword. For I have come to set a man against his father, etc."). This is not just consistent with an eschatological outlook – Mic 7:6 was drawn upon to describe the tribulation of the latter days – but further harmonizes with a biographical fact about Jesus – his own familial conflict. It contains, moreover, formal features characteristic of Jesus' speech (parallelism, the unexpected). So the conclusion that certain apocalyptic sayings go back to Jesus is not just a product of my premise: the final conclusion also fortifies the opening supposition.

The attribution to Jesus of units such as Luke 12:51–53 and 17:26–27 (both from Q) is further vindicated because it enables us to understand why his program exhibits so many striking parallels with world-wide millenarian movements. Like many Pacific cargo cults, Jewish messianic groups, Amerindian prophetic movements, and Christian sects looking for the end of the world, Jesus evidently did the following:

- addressed the disaffected or less fortunate in a period of social change that threatened traditional ways and symbolic universes; his movement indeed emerged in a time of aspiration for national independence
- understood the present and near future as times of suffering and/or catastrophe
- envisaged a comprehensive righting of wrongs and promised redemption through a reversal of current circumstances
- depicted that reversal as imminent
- engaged in evangelistic and revivalistic activities
- promoted egalitarianism
- divided the world into two camps: the just and the unjust
- broke hallowed taboos associated with religious custom
- replaced traditional familial and social bonds with fictive kin

- mediated the sacred through new channels
- demanded intense commitment and unconditional loyalty
- focused upon a charismatic leader
- understood his beliefs to be the product of special revelation
- took a passive political stance in expectation of a divinely-wrought deliverance
- expected a restored paradise that would return the ancestors
- insisted on the possibility of experiencing that utopia as a present reality
- grew out of a precursor movement

Some recent reconstructions of Jesus tend to eliminate the millenarian eschatology from the original tradition. And it is true that, after their deaths and sometimes even before, heroes often become gardens where apocryphal traditions get planted and thrive. But the elimination of millenarian eschatology from the earliest Jesus tradition is not plausible. Jesus' thought focused on the culmination of Israel's story and so his speech was dominated by the hope of salvation and the threat of judgment. His moral imperatives were an urgent plea for the spiritual reformation that was widely expected to herald the advent of the Day of the Lord. Jesus, in sum, was a Jewish visionary who demanded change in the face of the eschatological crisis and interpreted his own person and ministry in terms of scriptural fulfillment.[7] And his chief goal, as the last prophet in the cosmic drama, was to prepare his people for the eschatological finale.

7. Allison, *The Intertextual Jesus.*

# Jesus was not an Apocalyptic Prophet

**Part 1**
**The Debate**

Chapter 2
**Con**

Marcus Borg
John Dominic Crossan
Stephen Patterson

## MARCUS BORG

I admire Dale Allison's *Jesus of Nazareth: Millenarian Prophet.* I am impressed by how much he knows and how much he has read. His writing is lively and lucid, accomplishments too uncommon in the academic world. In my judgment, his sketch of Jesus as a "millenarian prophet" is the strongest contemporary scholarly case for an "apocalyptic Jesus," a phrase I will use as shorthand for seeing the historical Jesus within the paradigm of apocalyptic eschatology.

The apocalyptic Jesus dominated Jesus scholarship for much of the twentieth century. But in the last two decades, as Bob Miller has noted in his introduction, there has been a significant scholarly shift away from an apocalyptic Jesus to a non-apocalyptic Jesus. Perhaps a slight majority of scholars have made this shift, or perhaps the discipline is about equally divided. This development has generated a reaction among other scholars, and several have written book-length studies reaffirming the apocalyptic Jesus. In addition to Dale, they include E. P. Sanders, Bart Ehrman and Paula Fredriksen.

### Introduction

The question of whether Jesus is to be seen through the lens of apocalyptic eschatology has been with me all of my adult life.

Some thirty-five years ago, I was one of those seminarians to whom Dale refers in his book who went through "a sort of conversion experience"[1] that led me to embrace an apocalyptic Jesus.

---

1. Allison, *Jesus,* 38.

I first encountered the apocalyptic Jesus in Albert Schweitzer's *The Quest of the Historical Jesus*. The other scholars whom I read in my first New Testament course in seminary agreed: Rudolf Bultmann, Gunther Bornkamm, H. J. Tödt, W. G. Kümmel, and Joachim Jeremias. With variations of detail, all affirmed an apocalyptic Jesus. It was the mid-century consensus, dissented from by only a few scholars, mostly British.

I found the hypothesis persuasive and compelling. It seemed to account for so much. I was impressed by the claim (recently re-emphasized by Dale and others) that both John the Baptizer and Paul had an apocalyptic eschatology. The implication seemed obvious: if both Jesus' immediate predecessor and his earliest successor thought "the end" was at hand, then it made sense that Jesus thought so too.

Within the synoptic gospels, I was struck by the "coming Son of Man" sayings that spoke of a supernatural judge and rescuer coming on the clouds of heaven in the near future. They seemed to fit like a glove with passages about the imminence of the Kingdom of God. I was convinced.

But a few years later, under the influence of the late British scholar George Caird, my mind changed. My doctoral dissertation (completed in 1972) challenged the apocalyptic paradigm for interpreting the historical Jesus, and argued that a non-apocalyptic paradigm for seeing Jesus made more sense of more of the synoptic tradition. Because it was such a lonely position, I thought I was making a long-odds wager and might very well be wrong. But I also thought it a case worth making, and I have written much about it in the years since. It was the subject not only of my 1972 thesis, but also of my major revision of it published as *Conflict, Holiness and Politics in the Teachings of Jesus*. I have also written chapter-length articles on the subject.[2] Moreover, the non-apocalyptic paradigm shapes the sketch of Jesus I have drawn in several books.[3] And, to be candid, because I have written so much on this topic, it is difficult to say much that is new.

Thus, over the decades I have become more and more persuaded by the non-apocalyptic paradigm. I have been encouraged by a significant number of scholars who arrived independently at

---

2. Borg, "A Temperate Case" and "Jesus and Eschatology."
3. Borg, *Jesus: A New Vision*; *Meeting Jesus Again*; *The Meaning of Jesus*.

the same conclusion. When I joined the Jesus Seminar in the mid 1980s, I was surprised and delighted to discover that the majority of them (most of whom I had not previously met) also favored a non-apocalyptic framework.

## The Importance of Paradigm

As an advocate of a non-apocalyptic Jesus, and one whose work Dale critiques, I obviously disagree with him. But my point of departure in this chapter is not our disagreements, but a major and foundational agreement.

Namely, I agree with Dale's emphasis on the central importance of the "paradigm" through which we see the traditions about Jesus. As Dale puts it, "We do not come to our task with nothing more than the Jesus tradition, a knowledge of first-century history, and our criteria in hand."[4] Rather, we bring with us a "paradigm," "a matrix," "a primary frame of reference," a "gestalt," an "initial hypothesis" that arranges "data into coherent patterns."[5]

Our paradigm, he correctly emphasizes, affects our judgments about both historicity (what does and does not go back to Jesus) and interpretation (how we see the meaning of traditions we think do go back to Jesus). It shapes our perception of "*both* the *authenticity* of traditions and their *interpretation.*"[6] It affects our decisions about how "to construe the data – to interpret on the one hand, and to discard, on the other."[7]

With all of this, I agree. Indeed, the importance of paradigm for historical Jesus research has been a major theme of my own work, beginning with my doctoral thesis. It was essentially a paradigm argument. I argued that the "cornerstone" (paradigm) with which we begin our reconstruction of Jesus decisively shapes the resulting edifice, and that a non-apocalyptic cornerstone (paradigm) accommodates more of the traditions about Jesus than an apocalyptic one.

The conflict between an apocalyptic and non-apocalyptic Jesus is thus foundationally a paradigm conflict. We are dealing with dueling paradigms. When the issue is a choice between compet-

4. Allison, *Jesus*, 36.
5. Allison, *Jesus*, 36–39.
6. Allison, *Jesus*, 36, italics added.
7. Allison, *Jesus*, 37.

ing paradigms, there are two key questions: 1) What is the basis or foundation for generating the paradigm? 2) Which paradigm makes more comprehensive sense of the traditions about Jesus and enables us to see them as a compelling whole? Much of this chapter will address these questions.

## Some Preliminaries

Before turning to our competing paradigms, I make three comments about Dale's critique of my position that create a misleading impression of how I see things. They are also directly germane to the argument of this chapter.

First, his presentation of my case against the apocalyptic Jesus creates a misleading impression of the case that I do make. In his critique of my argument, he uses about half of the space[8] to analyze and reject Dom Crossan's argument (which I reported in a 1994 essay) that language about the "coming Son of Man" is weakly attested in the early layers of the tradition. Whether this part of Dale's critique is successful, I leave to Dom and others to decide.

What I wish to emphasize here is that I reported Dom's argument as additional support for an argument that I had already made *on other grounds* many years earlier. That is the case that Dale needs to undermine, not my corroborative use of Crossan. Because I have presented that fuller case in the writings I have already referred to, I will not present it again here, though parts of it will be integrated into the main body of this chapter.

Second and less seriously, in his critique of my paradigm, Dale argues that Jesus did indeed speak of repentance. His emphasis might imply that I don't think he did. But that is not the case. I think Jesus did preach repentance, and I have written about that in several places (this part of Dale's argument might better have been made against E. P. Sanders). Rather, my argument is the more specific claim: the *motive* for Jesus' preaching of repentance was *not* because time was short. To put it positively: Jesus did preach repentance, but not because he thought the end was near.

Of the three corrections, the third is most important. It concerns Dale's presentation of my "paradigm" or "gestalt" for seeing Jesus. Several times he uses the phrase "aphoristic sage" as short-

8. Allison, *Jesus*, 116–19.

hand for it.[9] He thereby reduces my multi-stroke paradigm for see-ing Jesus to a single stroke: "aphoristic sage."

I am puzzled by this. I cannot recall having used the phrase "aphoristic sage" in print (though I have used the word "sage," and I do think Jesus used aphorisms). And I am certain that I have never used the phrase as a shorthand summary of how I see Jesus. It might be good shorthand for how Burton Mack and Robert Funk see Jesus. But it is not a good summary of how I see Jesus.

Rather, my paradigm for seeing Jesus has consistently been a multi-stroke sketch. Sometimes I have spoken of a four-stroke sketch, sometimes a five-stroke sketch. That's because I sometimes combined the first two strokes into one. But my paradigm has always had five main elements. Because I have written much about this elsewhere, I here condense them to a sentence each.

1. Jesus was a "Spirit person" or "Jewish mystic," one for whom God or the sacred was an experiential reality, not simply an article of belief; I see this element as foundational for what else Jesus was.
2. He was a healer and exorcist; in terms of the number of such stories told about him, he is the most remarkable healer in the Jewish tradition.
3. He was an enlightened Jewish wisdom teacher who, like the authors of Job and Ecclesiastes, taught an unconventional wisdom, a way or path that led beyond conventional ways of seeing and living.
4. He was a social prophet (like Amos, Micah, Jeremiah, etc.) who indicted the domination system of his day in the name of the God whose passion is justice.
5. He was a movement initiator within Judaism; a remarkably egalitarian movement came into existence around him during his lifetime, and its most characteristic public activity was inclusive meal practice.

So, as we now turn to the topic of dueling paradigms, the two paradigms to compare are not "aphoristic sage" versus "millenar-ian prophet." Rather, they are "mystic-healer-wisdom teacher-social prophet-movement initiator" versus "millenarian prophet."

## Dueling Paradigms

Lest it seem unfair to summarize Dales' paradigm with one phrase while I get five, I add that his gestalt is fuller. It includes healer and movement initiator. It also includes "wisdom teacher." But,

9. See, for example, Allison, *Jesus*, 38, 96, 113, 129. See also above, p. 19.

to name two points to which I will return later, Dale's apocalyptic paradigm leads to a quite different understanding of Jesus' wisdom, and it seems to exclude Jesus being a social prophet.

Establishing a paradigm involves two stages: generating and confirming. The process of generation and confirmation is like the middle and final stages of detective work, to use an analogy I have used before.[10] After gathering potential evidence ("potential" because some of it may turn out not to be evidence), the detective forms a hunch, generating a paradigm for construing the evidence into a coherent whole.

The relationship between hunch/paradigm and evidence is reciprocal. The hunch/paradigm needs to be generated from the evidence; once generated, it affects how the evidence is seen. It affects what is considered to be evidence: data that looked like evidence but do not fit the hunch/paradigm need to be discarded or explained in some other way. It also affects the interpretation of the evidence.

The remaining stage of the process is, of course, confirming the hunch/paradigm. The test is obvious: how coherently and persuasively does the paradigm integrate the evidence? And how much of what looked like evidence needs to be left out? And does that evidence look suspect, or does it seem so solid that the process of hunching a paradigm must begin over again?

### Generating a Paradigm: Foundations

Dale generates his hunch in a distinctive way. Specifically, he does not use the sayings and deeds of Jesus as part of the foundation for his paradigm. Rather, he generates his paradigm "prior to and independently" of his "evaluation of the historicity of individual items" in the traditions about Jesus.[11] His subordination of Jesus' sayings and deeds to the apocalyptic paradigm is emphatic. After citing his reasons for affirming an apocalyptic Jesus, he says:

> Further, this result is sufficiently forceful that, were the sayings attributed to Jesus to suggest some other conclusion, the correct inference would probably not be that Jesus was not an eschatological prophet but rather that the sayings tradition is unreliable.[12]

---

10. Borg, "Jesus and Eschatology," 80; *The Meaning of Jesus*, 237–38.
11. Allison, *Jesus*, 39.
12. Allison, *Jesus*, 44.

In this respect, he differs from those who pioneered the apocalyptic paradigm a hundred years ago. For both Johannes Weiss
and Albert Schweitzer, the apocalyptic Jesus was grounded in the
sayings of Jesus. Two categories of sayings were foundational:

- sayings about "the Son of Man" who is coming to judge the world
  and/or rescue the followers of Jesus in the near future.
- sayings about the imminent coming of the kingdom of God.

Weiss and Schweitzer took the theme of imminent supernatural intervention found in both those categories of sayings and
attached it to all the kingdom sayings, and then to all of the material that speaks of crisis or urgency.

But Dale generates his apocalyptic paradigm without using the
sayings of Jesus. Without them, what are his foundations? He lists
five.[13]

1. Jesus' vision of the future is most likely continuous with his most
   prominent predecessor and his most prominent successor; both John
   the Baptizer and Paul had an apocalyptic eschatology.
2. Resurrection language is apocalyptic language.
3. The death of Jesus is narrated with eschatological language.
4. Apocalyptic eschatology was widespread in the first century.
5. Several New Testament texts compare Jesus to eschatological figures
   like John the Baptist, Theudas, and Judas the Galilean.

For the sake of compactness, I reduce these to three without, I
trust, shortchanging Dale's argument. Number four, I suggest, is
without evidentiary weight. That apocalyptic eschatology was
widespread does not tell us that Jesus proclaimed it, any more
than the fact that armed revolution was "in the air" in the Jewish
homeland in the first century suggests that Jesus advocated it.

Number five, I suggest, is a variant of number one: Jesus was
like John the Baptizer. The cases of Theudas and Judas the
Galilean do not count for much. Though Theudas expected imminent supernatural deliverance, it is not clear that Judas the
Galilean did. What they share with Jesus is not primarily apocalyptic expectation, but that they were movement leaders whose
movements were quashed by established authority.

Thus the first three reasons are Dale's foundations for generat-

13. Allison, *Jesus*, 39–44. See also above, pp. 20–24.

ing his paradigm. How solid are they? I treat them in reverse order.

To begin with the third, that New Testament authors write about the death of Jesus in eschatological language tells us nothing about Jesus' own eschatology. Some of that language is used in the Hebrew Bible to refer to historical and not apocalyptic events. Moreover, from the post-Easter vantage point of the early Christian community, Jesus' death and resurrection marked the turning of the ages, so it is not surprising that they used eschatological language to express this conviction.

His second foundation, as I understand it, concerns the early community's interpretation of what happened to Jesus after his death as "resurrection." Dale asks, in effect, why would the community use an eschatological term like resurrection to speak about this? His answer: the most likely reason is that Jesus himself had been using the language of apocalyptic eschatology, including the notion that the general resurrection was imminent.

It seems to me equally plausible to imagine a different scenario. I begin with the Easter experience. I take very seriously the phenomenology of early Christian religious experience: after Jesus' death some of his followers really experienced him as a living reality and continuing presence. Whatever one does ontologically with these experiences, I think his followers had such experiences. Moreover, and very importantly, something about these experiences also led to the affirmation "Jesus is Lord," "raised to God's right hand." Easter is not simply about the conviction that Jesus lives, but that he is Lord. Easter is not primarily about apparitions, or survival of death, or "ghost stories." Easter is about Jesus' vindication and lordship. Indeed, "raised to God's right hand" may be earlier than "raised from the dead," and may also express the central meaning better.

Now, how are people in a first-century Jewish milieu going to talk about their conviction that Jesus lives and has been raised to God's right hand? The language of resuscitation won't do, nor will ghost stories. But the language of resurrection is immediately at hand. Thus I think the use of resurrection language is generated by the nature of the Easter experience, and not to be seen as a reason for saying that Jesus expected the general resurrection to be imminent.

Dale's first foundation depends upon continuity between the apocalyptic expectation of John the Baptizer, Paul, and Jesus. Undermining this foundation requires only two counter-claims. There is space only to name them, not argue them.

The first counter-claim: Jesus differed from John on apocalyptic eschatology. Virtually every scholar agrees that Jesus and John differed in some significant ways. Why should we assume continuity of apocalyptic eschatology? The case needs to be made, not assumed.

The second counter-claim: the apocalyptic eschatology of Paul and early Christianity arose in the community after Easter. It originated in the deep conviction shared by Jesus' followers that the turning of the ages had happened and was happening. They believed that God had acted decisively, first, in the teachings and actions of the historical Jesus; second, in God's vindication of Jesus at Easter; and third, in God's sending of the Spirit at Pentecost. Easter is shorthand for their conviction that God had raised Jesus to God's right hand so that he not only lived but had become Lord; Pentecost is shorthand for the experience of the Spirit in the community. Both of these experiences, spoken of as resurrection and the outpouring of the Spirit, had eschatological associations: they would happen in the last days. Thus, in the experience and conviction of early Christians, the decisive transformation of life on earth had begun. No wonder many of them thought the apocalyptic consummation was near.

In addition, two particular historical events in the decades after Easter probably contributed to the community's sense that the end was near. Both involved threats to the temple in Jerusalem.

In the early 40s, the Roman emperor Caligula issued an order to erect a statue of himself in the temple. Caligula's plan generated massive Jewish protest demonstrations and threatened to result in war. His death before the order could be carried out ended the crisis. But the crisis called to mind a time two centuries earlier when another pagan emperor had erected a statue of Zeus in the temple, an event called "the desolating sacrilege" or "abomination of desolation" in the apocalyptic scenario in the second half of the book of Daniel.

A generation later, in the year 70, the Jewish people experienced their single greatest catastrophe in ancient times: the devastating Roman response to the Jewish revolt of 66. Roman legions reconquered the Jewish homeland and Jerusalem, with enormous loss of Jewish life, and then destroyed both Jerusalem and the temple.

Both of these events are likely to have intensified apocalyptic expectation among Jews, including Christian Jews. In particular, the Jewish apocalyptic books of Baruch and 4 Ezra both respond to the events of 70. Mark, our earliest canonical gospel, reflects

the circumstances of the year 70, most clearly in the "little apocalypse" of Mark 13. Indeed, all of the canonical gospels were written after the "apocalyptic event" of the Jewish war against Rome
and its aftermath. Thus I think there is strong evidence for heightened apocalyptic expectation during the decades during which the
traditions about Jesus took shape.

To return to the main point: in short, Dale locates the apocalyptic expectation of early Christianity in the pre-Easter message
of Jesus. I locate the apocalyptic expectation of early Christianity
in the post-Easter community.

I want to emphasize that my analysis thus far neither refutes
Dale's case nor points to mine as being stronger. My purpose has
been more limited: to show that it is not difficult to imagine a
plausible scenario for the apocalyptic expectation of early
Christianity developing after Easter rather than deriving from
Jesus. These two scenarios are, of course, the competing paradigms
that we are discussing.

I also emphasize that without the sayings and deeds tradition,
both scenarios/paradigms are equally plausible. Or, to say the
same thing differently, without the sayings and deeds tradition,
both scenarios/paradigms are equally inconclusive. In short, I
don't think a paradigm (apocalyptic or otherwise) can be established independently of the particularities (the sayings and deeds)
of the Jesus tradition.

Here it is instructive to refer to another scholar who, like Dale,
seeks to establish an apocalyptic understanding of Jesus without
using the sayings tradition. E. P. Sanders' argument that Jesus was
a prophet of temple restoration eschatology is well-known. But in
order to affirm not simply that Jesus warned of the temple's
destruction but also of its restoration (which is essential for his
case), Sanders has to appeal to an alleged saying of Jesus: namely,
a hypothetical saying presupposed by the accusation of Jesus'
opponents that he had spoken of replacing the present temple
with a new one. Sanders needs the saying to make his case. The
point: I do not think one can establish a paradigm without the
sayings tradition.

In my own work, the foundations for my multi-stroke sketch
of Jesus come from the cumulative impression created by the particularities of early layers of the Jesus tradition. They are generated from sayings, deeds, and narratives, seen within the
framework of a cross-cultural typology of religious figures.

### Confirming a Paradigm: Comprehensiveness and Persuasiveness

So I turn to the stage of confirming a paradigm. Here there are two questions, flowing out of the twofold function of paradigms. First, a paradigm functions to include and exclude material. Thus the first question concerns *comprehensiveness*. How much of the relevant data (mostly found in the synoptic gospels) can each paradigm accommodate? Secondly, a paradigm also functions as a lens through which what is included is seen. Thus its adequacy is judged not only by its comprehensiveness but also by the kind of "sense" it makes of the material, its *persuasiveness*. As a lens, which paradigm makes the most persuasive sense of the material?

*Comprehensiveness.* Dale's apocalyptic paradigm and my non-apocalyptic paradigm are both quite comprehensive. Neither of us needs to exclude very much, though what we do need to exclude is different and how we see what is included differs significantly. As I see it, his paradigm requires that he exclude what I call "social prophet" traditions. Whether he would exclude more, I leave up to him.

My non-apocalyptic paradigm obviously needs to exclude texts that require an apocalyptic reading. They are surprisingly few. Indeed, the textual basis for assigning an apocalyptic eschatology to Jesus is very slim.

The list of texts that do require such a reading (and which I must therefore assign to the post-Easter community) is short:

1. The relatively few sayings about the coming Son of Man. Though there have been scholarly attempts to read these in a non-temporal way and/or as referring to an historical event (most recently by N. T. Wright), I am not persuaded. I see them as "second coming" sayings, and as expressions of imminent apocalyptic eschatology.
2. One kingdom saying, Mark 9:1: "Truly I say to you, there are some of you standing here who will not taste death before they see the Kingdom of God come with power." If Mark 1:15 is to be understood in light of Mark 9:1, it also is an expression of apocalyptic eschatology. But if removed from its Markan context, Mark 1:15 need not be read this way.
3. Much of the Matthean redaction of Jesus' parables and sayings. Matthew contains more "last judgment" material than any other gospel.

It is important to note that a surprisingly large number of synoptic texts are neutral regarding imminent apocalyptic expectation. Most of the kingdom of God sayings fall into this neutral category. To pray for the coming of the kingdom does not imply that the apocalyptic kingdom is temporally imminent. So also, to proclaim that the kingdom is "near" or "at hand" need not imply temporal apocalyptic imminence.

Similarly, most of the very numerous "threat sayings" in the synoptic tradition are neutral regarding imminent apocalyptic expectation. To explain, I summarize a statistical analysis from my thesis and *Conflict, Holiness and Politics*. I divided the synoptic threat-sayings into categories. Twenty threats are peculiar to Matthew, and most of these threaten eternal punishment. If Matthew were the basis for discerning whether or not Jesus had an apocalyptic eschatology, our answer would almost certainly be yes.

But the other fifty-three threat sayings are quite different. They fall into two primary categories. Twenty-one are threats with unidentifiable content: the threat is left in the metaphorical language of the saying or parable. Crisis is at hand; *something* is threatening, but *what* is not specified. Thirty-two are threats with identifiable content. Of these, nine have a "taken away/given to others" pattern. Eleven refer to war and/or destruction of the temple and Jerusalem. Only twelve refer to the final judgment.

And even speaking about the last judgment does not in itself imply that it is imminent. When Jesus warned his hearers that long-dead Gentiles would fare better in the last judgment than "this generation," he did not say that the last judgment was to come while "this generation" was alive (Luke 11:31–32; see also Luke 10:13–14). This warning only says that when the last judgment comes, this is what it will be like. So also in the parable of the sheep and goats: Matthew's placement of it in chapter 25 suggests that the last judgment is imminent. But apart from that redactional setting, the parable does not imply imminence. Rather, its point is that the criterion God will use at the judgment (when it comes) will be deeds of compassion.

To summarize how I incorporate themes that are commonly seen as pointing to apocalyptic eschatology:

1. I think Jesus did speak of judgment. But I see the judgments as those of a social prophet.
2. I think Jesus did speak of repentance – though not in the sense of individuals preparing for the last judgment, but in the sense in which the social prophets of Israel spoke of repentance.
3. I think Jesus did speak of the resurrection of the dead – but as a threat

to "this generation." That is, his point was not, "It's soon, and you'd better be ready," but "When it happens, it will be very different from what you expect."

4. I think Jesus did threaten the destruction of the temple, in both prophetic threat oracles and the prophetic act of overturning the tables of the moneychangers. Moreover, he indicted the temple not because it represented Judaism, but because it represented the native domination system.

To bring this section on comprehensiveness to a close by repeating its primary point: very few synoptic sayings require an apocalyptic reading in order to make sense. Moreover, many that sound apocalyptic (kingdom sayings, threat sayings, last judgment sayings) sound that way because imminent expectation has been imported from outside the saying. In particular, seeing most of the threat sayings as pointing to apocalyptic eschatology comes from an habituated way of seeing generated by the dominance of the apocalyptic paradigm over the last century.

Thus, regarding apocalyptic eschatology, all I need to assign to the post-Easter community are the coming Son of man sayings (which I understand as second coming of Jesus sayings); Mark 9:1 (which fits well with the notion that the gospel of Mark, written around the year 70, reflects intensified apocalyptic expectation), and a considerable amount of Matthew's redaction.

*Persuasiveness.* As noted earlier, a paradigm functions not only to include and exclude but also as a lens through which we see what is included. Thus we judge a paradigm's adequacy and explanatory power not simply by its comprehensiveness but also by its persuasiveness as a lens: what the relevant data look like within its way of seeing, the kind of "sense" it makes of the material. Thus the question: which paradigm makes the most persuasive sense of the material?

This question moves us into the most subjective part of the historical process. Though all historical work is to some degree subjective (for it is always an individual historian who makes the judgments), some parts of the process involve appeals to somewhat objective data and criteria. But "persuasive sense" always means persuasive to somebody. Obviously, what is persuasive to me is not persuasive to Dale, and vice versa. So in this area perhaps the appeal is to "intersubjectivity" – to the judgment of readers about which reading makes more persuasive sense.

I begin by suggesting a spectrum of three paradigms for seeing the historical Jesus. As I do so, I will also use the term *gestalt,* a useful German word that means roughly "configuration," or "way of seeing the whole."

Each paradigm produces a gestalt of Jesus – a way of construing the traditions about Jesus as a whole. At one end of the spectrum is a non-apocalyptic paradigm, producing a non-apocalyptic gestalt. The second and third paradigms are both apocalyptic. Both lead to an apocalyptic gestalt of Jesus. But they differ in the role they assign to Jesus' alleged apocalyptic expectation. The second paradigm (the middle of the spectrum) sees such expectation as *secondary*, producing the gestalt of secondary apocalyptic. The third paradigm (the other end of the spectrum) sees such expectation as *primary*, producing the gestalt of primary apocalyptic.

> **Paradigm One: The Non-Apocalyptic Gestalt.** This is what I have been arguing for, of course: Jesus did not have an apocalyptic eschatology. Apocalyptic expectation in the gospels and the rest of the New Testament is "second coming of Jesus" eschatology. It does not go back to Jesus himself.
>
> **Paradigm Two: Secondary Apocalyptic Gestalt.** Here it is affirmed that, in addition to whatever else Jesus was doing and teaching, he thought that God would soon intervene to vindicate or complete what Jesus had begun. But apocalyptic conviction was not the primary energy driving his mission or shaping his teaching. Rather, it is one element in a fuller understanding of Jesus.
>
> **Paradigm Three: Primary Apocalyptic Gestalt.** This, of course, is the opposite pole from the first option. Not only did Jesus expect that God would soon intervene in a dramatic fashion to bring in the "end time" events, but this conviction was central for him. It animated his mission and pervasively shaped his message.

Assessing the persuasiveness of Dale's paradigm involves, among other things, clarity about whether he is advocating paradigm two or paradigm three. If he is advocating paradigm two (apocalyptic as secondary), then his understanding of Jesus might not be significantly different from what Dom and I advocate.

Suppose, for example, that Dale were willing to affirm that Dom is right that Jesus' mission centered in free healing (and thus immediacy of access to God) and open commensality (and thus an egalitarian social vision very different from hierarchical social visions, whether Roman or Jewish), *and* that Jesus *also* expected the imminent apocalyptic intervention of God. Or suppose that he were willing to affirm that I am right that Jesus was a healer, wisdom teacher, social prophet, movement founder, and maybe even a mystic, *and* that Jesus *also* expected imminent apocalyptic intervention. If this were his argument, then I would say that our difference is very specific and relatively minor. We are disagreeing about one element of Jesus' vision. Or was Jesus *primarily* a millenarian prophet? This is the question of secondary versus primary apocalyptic.

For two reasons, my hunch is that Dale is an advocate of paradigm three, in which apocalyptic expectation is primary rather than secondary (he must speak for himself, of course). His summary of the particulars of Jesus' eschatological vision points in this direction: Jesus as a millenarian prophet expected the restoration of Israel, the great tribulation, the final judgment, the resurrection of the dead, and all of this soon.[14] His use of "millenarian prophet" as a paradigm also suggests so. A paradigm is a primary lens.

The difference between the second and third ways of seeing apocalyptic is important. If apocalyptic expectation is secondary, then such expectation is one element in Jesus' message. But if it is primary, then it becomes the lens through which we must see the whole picture of Jesus' mission and message, not simply one of its elements.

Let me illustrate the effect upon "the whole" with several examples of how paradigm three — hereafter called in shorthand "primary apocalyptic" — affects the way one sees the wisdom teaching of Jesus. To Dale, if he holds this position, and to anybody who holds position three, I suggest reflection about the following texts and themes, all central to the wisdom teaching of Jesus. Each example also includes a rhetorical question addressed to those who hold this position.

*The Beatitudes.* Jesus declares the poor, the hungry, the weeping, and the persecuted to be blessed. Why are they blessed? For primary apocalyptic: because the last judgment and the great reversal are coming soon. About this one may ask: Is that why the poor, and so forth, are blessed?

*Teachings about wealth.* Divest yourself of wealth and give to the poor. Why? For primary apocalyptic: because the last judgment is at hand. But is that why one should give to the poor — so that one will be rewarded at the last judgment?

*Compassion and mercy.* Why be compassionate? For primary

14. Allison, *Jesus*, 129–51.

apocalyptic: because the last judgment is coming soon. Similarly, be merciful to others so that God will be merciful to you in the last judgment. But is that why one should be compassionate and merciful?

*The importance of seeing.* Many of Jesus' sayings and deeds have to do with the importance of seeing. For primary apocalyptic, what is this seeing about? Presumably about seeing that the time is near. But is that what seeing means, and is that why it's important?

*The last will be first, the humble will be exalted.* The apocalyptic paradigm stresses that in the last judgment, everything will be reversed: those who are last will be first, those who have been humbled will be exalted. But is that why we are to make ourselves "last" – so that we can be "first" in the judgment? Are we to humble ourselves so that we will be exalted in the judgment? Is that what this teaching is about?

*The Prodigal Son.* What does this mean within the paradigm of primary apocalyptic? That following the rules (like the older brother did) isn't what God will be looking for, but repentance in time for the last judgment? Or is the parable really about something else?

*The Good Samaritan.* A major point of the parable is "be a neighbor" by acting compassionately. Is it important to be a neighbor and act compassionately because the judgment is at hand? Is that why we should act thus?

*Teaching about family.* For primary apocalyptic, family ties and responsibilities are relativized because the apocalypse is at hand. But is this why Jesus says what he says about family?

*Teaching about honor.* For primary apocalyptic, honor does not matter if the judgment is soon. But is this why preoccupation with honor is foolish?

*Parables about treasure hidden in a field and a pearl of great value.* For primary apocalyptic, presumably these two brief parables mean something like, "Whatever you have to give up to prepare for the judgment is worth it." But is this what these arresting parables are about?

*Teaching about "the way."* What is "the way" or "the path" which Jesus taught? Is it the path of preparation for the last judgment? Or is it a way/path that has nothing to do with an imminent final judgment?

*Teaching about purity.* True purity is inward, not outward. Within the paradigm of primary apocalyptic, does this mean we will be judged at the last judgment on the basis of inner purity, not outward observance? Is this why the distinction between inner purity and outer purity matters?

Let's move beyond the wisdom teaching of Jesus. For primary apocalyptic, what is the significance of Jesus' inclusive meal practice with marginalized people and outcasts? Did it mean simply, "When the judgment and the messianic banquet arrive, these folks will be included, so I'm including them now?" Or does his inclusive meal practice have a different motive and meaning?

Consider also how we might think of the relationship between Jesus and God's justice. Was Jesus (1) advocating God's justice in this world, or (2) promising post-apocalyptic justice? Primary apocalyptic suggests the second (and this seems to be what Dale is saying). If so, then Jesus is another mistaken proclaimer of "God's going to fix everything, and soon." But if Dale were to say, "It's not an either-or choice, but both," then I would want to ask, In what proportion? How important is each in your understanding of Jesus? The more importance one gives to the first, the more one has moved away from primary apocalyptic.

Though more examples could be given, I have neither the space nor the intent to be comprehensive. Rather, my purpose has been to show that a large amount of Jesus' teaching seems to have little to do with apocalyptic eschatology. It makes better sense apart from an apocalyptic framework, and seems to have its origin in convictions and perceptions other than "the apocalypse is at hand."

Moreover, when we do presume the paradigm of primary apocalyptic, the effect is a "flattening" of Jesus' teaching. It becomes one-dimensional, almost banal. The great reversal is coming, and that's why the poor are blessed, why the humble will be exalted, why the first will be last, why you should give to the poor, why family and honor don't matter, why you should follow the path of Jesus. The apocalyptic relativization of everything reduces the paradoxical, provocative and sometimes enigmatic teaching of Jesus to a simple-minded, "Repent, the judgment is at hand."

If Dale should object that his position does not require that all or most of Jesus' teaching and activity was apocalyptically motivated, I would ask a very simple question: How much is not? A little? A lot? For those who affirm an apocalyptic paradigm, this is the question of primary versus secondary apocalyptic.

In short, it seems to me that, through the lens of primary apocalyptic, the teaching of Jesus looks like much less than it is. For
me, the problem with the paradigm of primary apocalyptic is not
that it makes Jesus seem weird and mistaken, but that it makes
him seem banal. Let me add that it is not simply my commitment
to Jesus and to Christianity that leads me to reject the notion that
Jesus' message and vision were banal. There is much evidence that
his message was far from banal, indeed that many people found it
to be provocative, disturbing, and subversive.

So I do not think Jesus had an apocalyptic eschatology. Or if
he did, it was secondary, and not primary. I don't think it was the
animating vision generating his mission. My own hunch is that
his animating vision flowed out of his experience of the sacred,
his familiarity with the traditions of Israel (whether only in oral or
also in written form, I do not know), and his observation of the
conditions of peasant life.

As a wisdom teacher, I think he taught a way or a path that pro-
vided immediacy of access to God, one that was open to marginalized peasants and outcasts. As a social prophet proclaiming the
kingdom of God, I think he was a radical critic of the domination
system of his day, and that he threatened it with destruction in
the name of God. There is urgency and crisis in his words and
deeds. But I think it is the urgency of a social prophet, not the
urgency of apocalyptic eschatology. The movement which he ini-
tiated, whose meal practice emphasized both sharing food and
breaking social boundaries, embodied his social vision of what
Israel was to be. But I don't think his passion was about preparing
people for the last judgment.

And so the questions remain. Which of these paradigms – the
paradigm of primary apocalyptic, or a non-apocalyptic paradigm
– better accommodates the data that we find in the synoptic
gospels? And beyond that, which paradigm better enables us to
see "the whole" in a way that accounts for the persuasive and compelling power that these traditions have had through the centuries?

## JOHN DOMINIC CROSSAN

Surely if Jesus was, as so many have held, an eschatological prophet
who lived in the imaginative world of the apocalypses, we should not
expect much consistency from him, for the *essential irrationality* of

apocalyptic is manifest from the history of messianic and millenarian movements. . . .

Jesus the millenarian prophet, like all millenarian prophets, was *wrong*: reality has taken no notice of his imagination. . . .

And yet, despite everything, for those who have ears to hear, Jesus, the millenarian herald of judgment and salvation, says the only things worth saying, for *his dream is the only one worth dreaming*. . . . If in the end there is no good God to calm this sea of troubles, to raise the dead, and to give good news to the poor, then this is indeed a tale told by an idiot, signifying nothing.[15]

Responding to your book is a special pleasure for me, Dale, because you are both clear and precise in proposing your own position but also careful and fair in summarizing those with whom you disagree. A decade ago such an opening sentence would not have been necessary, but the ethics of the current Jesus wars mean that very seldom now do I recognize my own books in the summaries of their reviewers nor my own voice in the criticisms of my colleagues. When I say special pleasure, therefore, I am not just being ritually polite but sincerely grateful for the presence of accuracy and the absence of contempt in your writing.

My reply has two points but the second is by far the more important for me. I have thought very seriously about omitting the former one lest it distract from the latter but I include it here in far less space and ask you to consider it accordingly. You may, from my point of view and for the purposes of this book, omit any answer to *Methodology* should space be limited and *Eschatology* require all that is available.

First, under *Methodology*, I counter your criticisms of my methodology,[16] especially if and when I think you have misunderstood it. But I do this almost in passing because that is not where I want our major discussion to take place. Second, under *Eschatology*, I offer what I hope will move the debate forward. I presume this is not the confrontation of two implacable and immovable positions and so this is what I want to do in that second but, for me, much more significant section. I intend to accept (*dato non concesso*, to be sure) your full and entire position on the apocalyptic continuity from John, through Jesus, into Paul, Q, and Mark. And also, while we are at it, on the non-metaphoricity

15. Allison, *Jesus*, 4, 218, 219 (italics added).
16. Allison, *Jesus*, 10–33.

of apocalyptic or millenarian language (*dnc* again) across that continuity. Then, within your own framework, I will propose emphases and priorities that you did not make (or made only in passing). I will argue that such discriminations are mandated by the history *you* record, the history of a millenarian movement, wrong like all the others before and after it (at least so far), but evincing one rather striking feature: *as it got wronger, it got stronger.*

## Methodology

This is not so much a full response as an indication of how I would conduct a more appropriately adequate one if time, space, and, most especially, my present emphases, allowed it. *Material*, for me, precedes *method*. In other words, earlier decisions about the nature of the gospel traditions became presuppositions for my work on the historical Jesus. By earlier I mean, first, the source-work of scholarly ancestors and, second, my own redaction-work which both tested their theses and pushed their limits. If, for example, I had become convinced that Matthew, Mark, Luke, and John, even granting their accepted dates, were four *independent* accounts of Jesus, my method for reconstructing the historical Jesus would have been completely different. In that case, I would have been primarily impressed with *fourfold* agreement on anything.

What overwhelmingly impressed me then and what has remained overwhelmingly operative beneath all my later work is this conclusion: the tradition of written texts from Mark and Q, through Matthew and Luke, into John (as dependent on them for *at least* its narrative frames of Baptist and Passion-Resurrection), is an intensely absorptive tradition, with later texts attempting to swallow earlier ones whole, with later texts intensely and creatively rewriting former ones. That is neither a dogmatic presupposition nor a theological affirmation but is simply a first historical conclusion (thereafter, an historical presupposition) about the nature of the intracanonical gospel tradition. And this is the immediate second one. If things were such with written texts across twenty-five years (say, 70 to 95), did Mark operate any differently, any more or less creatively, with pre-Markan oral and scribal traditions? And what of the layers, sources, or data before that? What was happening across forty pre-Markan years? Maybe, of course, tradition was handed on unchanged until Mark took it down accurately and uncreatively. But, for one point, that was not what attempting to do redactional criticism on Mark had taught me. And, for another, a comparison of Mark and the Q Gospel indicated two texts equally but differently redactional and creative. That gave me a second historical conclusion (thereafter, a historical presupposition), that it is necessary, *in such an absorptive tradition*, to attempt a push-back to the earliest materials. That is not a *general* theoretical position based on the presumption that earliest is most accurate. It is a *particular* methodological discipline required to probe the origins of that precise tradition.

I place those two presuppositions up front as preamble because, before I had any hypotheses about the character of the historical Jesus, I had hypotheses about the character of the gospel tradition. Materials preceded methods preceded conclusions. It was, for specific example, a study of the parables tradition that gave me my first hypothesis about Jesus, namely, that he was *eschatological but not apocalyptic*. That has been my explicit position for over thirty years.[17] To test that hypothesis, to understand non-apocalyptic eschatology positively and not just negatively, and then to name it (prophetic or sapiential or ethical eschatology?) has been the burden of my historical Jesus research across those decades. I have never, ever said that Jesus was non-eschatological. In brief response to your main points:

*Scholarly Diversity.* This is simply a misunderstanding of my position which was about inventory and not about interpretation. I have no problem with hermeneutical diversity, have spent my entire life in its midst, am quite at home within it, and never expect it to disappear. My purpose in *The Historical Jesus* was to start a major debate on method among my peers. How does one get the data base to be used for reconstruction and interpretation (however diverse)? If we cannot even agree on inventory, what use is there in arguing about interpretation? We are simply looking at different texts.

*Stratification.* My strata dates are important only in their relative succession (what I called the "sequence of strata"). I could call those layers: pre-canonical (30–70 C.E.), intracanonical (70–95 C.E.), and post or para-canonical (95–160 C.E.) or even, more simply, pre-Mark (30–70 C.E.) and post-Mark (70–150 C.E.). My method was especially concerned with looking at what was there

17. See, for example, Crossan, *In Parables*, 25–27.

before Mark, namely and especially, the authentic Pauline letters and the Q Gospel which I took as dated to the 50s. You ask, What "if one were to put Q in the 60s instead of 40s or 50s"?[18] Then, with Paul in the first stratum, the Q Gospel and Mark are in the second stratum. So what? My "primary stratum" shifts from first alone to first plus second (Paul, Q Gospel, Mark). Numbers would change, of course, but conclusions would not. If, however and for example, Matthew were dated to the 50s, everything would have to be redone (including the synoptic problem!).

*Multiple, Single, and Double Attestation.* Here, as with *Scholarly Diversity* above, you have misunderstood my point (I think). I have never argued and do not think that "the more attestation something has the more confident we can be about its origin" or that "the popularity of a complex bespeaks authenticity."[19] I focused on multiple independent attestation *within the primary stratum*, that is, on at least double independent attestation of a unit found within a document dated (in effect) before Mark, for example, something in Paul or the Q Gospel and independently elsewhere.

*Tradition-histories and the Burden of Proof.* You state that "the burden of proof should always be on the one making an argument."[20] That sounds better the less one thinks about it. First, it is itself an argument and therefore needs proof and not just assertion. Second, if accepted, *it applies to gospel writers even before gospel exegetes.* It is not just a question of whether we prove Jesus did not say this or that but whether a gospel writer proved that he did. My own use of the phrase was far less sweeping. I was simply saying that, for me, anything with double independent attestation in the primary stratum was in until and unless I could prove it out to my own satisfaction. My burden, nobody else's.

*Uncertainties.* You ask "Where are all the question marks?"[21] First, at the start of *The Historical Jesus*, in attempting a self-conscious methodology and in making clear that everything depends on it (results depend on methods, methods depend on materials), I place the whole under question-mark. Second, at the end, by insisting on the word "reconstruction" rather than "quest" or "search" I do the same again. You have found the historical Jesus, once and for all forever. You have small question marks but no

18. Allison, *Jesus*, 16.
19. Allison, *Jesus*, 21, 24.
20. Allison, *Jesus*, 27.
21. Allison, *Jesus*, 32.

big ones. I had reconstructed the historical Jesus as best I could do for here and now. I said so explicitly: "This book is one scholar's reconstruction."[22] I do not scatter small question marks throughout my work. I put big ones in Prologue and Epilogue.

## Eschatology

At this point I bracket completely that prior debate about methodology to move exclusively within your own position on the apocalyptic Jesus. I accept it for here and now as fully and honestly as I can (*dnc*, as always). This is not some sort of devious strategy but an attempt to see what is most fundamentally at stake in our disagreement. It is most important for me that we debate on that level in this book (other times, other places, other details).

### (1) Thesis

*Apocalyptic Matrix.* You locate what biblical scholars term apocalypticism within the wider cross-cultural phenomenon known to comparative religion as millenarianism, a phenomenon often *in*dependent of Jewish or Christians sources.[23] I agree on that fuller matrix. I made that same equation in *The Historical Jesus*, but, although I used some of the general works you cite (Worsley, Thrupp, and especially Wilson, for example), you have read far, far more individual studies than I have. In any case, no disagreement here (*dato et concesso*, this time).

*Apocalyptic Continuity.* Your following argument, while not absolutely logical is surely persuasively common-sensical. There was apocalypticism before Jesus in John the Baptist, there was apocalypticism after Jesus in Paul, Q, and Mark. Furthermore, we find apocalyptic warnings on Jesus' own lips all over the synoptic gospels. It is, therefore, at least most likely, as you say, that Jesus was an apocalyptic visionary, a millenarian ascetic, an eschatological prophet.[24] In this response, I situate myself within that quite reasonable hypothesis (*dato non concesso*, this time).

*Apocalyptic Language.* You argue for apocalyptic language as primarily if not exclusively literal in its own intentionality.[25] It is accepted metaphorically or at least with increasing metaphoricity

---

22. Crossan, *Historical Jesus*, 424.
23. Allison, *Jesus*, 78–94.
24. Allison, *Jesus*, 39–44.
25. Allison, *Jesus*, especially 152–69.

only after its literal expectations falter and fail. You take that as apologetical damage control. We should accept apocalypticism literally "even if this puts us in the disagreeable company of modern fundamentalists."[26] We should not translate it metaphorically "like others who have offered us a more theologically convenient Jesus."[27]

## (2) Antithesis

Accepting your position and working absolutely within it, I have the following immediate problem. You assert very clearly and very honestly that "Jesus the millenarian prophet, like all millenarian prophets, was wrong."[28] You use no subterfuge, that, for example, by "imminent" or "within this generation" he or they meant sometime within some generation maybe even two thousand years from now. But, for Jesus-based earliest Christianity, as I said aphoristically above, the longer they were wrong, the longer they got strong. That is my problem: longer, wronger, stronger. Why? As the decades of the first hundred years passed without millenarian consummation, tiny ripples of surprise appear on the surface of the tradition, but I see no evidence of profound doubt or massive loss of faith. I do *not* find what I might have expected: profound defensive strategies, desperate explanatory interpretations, but, despite them, slow and steady attrition in faith. I would have expected, in other words, a steadily decreasing number of converts and communities and I find instead a steadily increasing number of both converts and communities. I presume, by the way, Dale, that you would agree with this paragraph.

I am not making any cryptic claim for the "uniqueness" of either historical Jesus or earliest Christianity. A careful study of all your cross-cultural millenarian parallels might indicate why, how, where, when, etc., such movements survive, grow, and eventually develop into worldwide religions. Lacking that for the moment, I simply note that because of or despite its being "wrong," Jesus-based earliest Christianity was increasingly successful in its missionary movement. I am, as you will realize, taking your own *total* thesis seriously and this precludes certain easy outs.

First, I do not suggest that the apocalyptic historical Jesus was

26. Allison, *Jesus*, 164.
27. Allison, *Jesus*, 166.
28. Allison, *Jesus*, 218.

millenarian and therefore wrong, but that having recognized the problem, earliest Christianity changed, became non-apocalyptic, and was right. That would deny *your* argument for fundamental apocalyptic continuity across most of Christianity's first century. Second, respecting *your* literal apocalyptic language claims, I do not suggest that metaphorical continuity solves the problem. Besides, even or especially a metaphor must be a metaphor for something. So we would still have to ask what that something is. Finally, I cannot simply say that Jesus' resurrection explains it all, that Jesus' resurrection is what made, and even alone what made, Christianity a successful missionary religion.

Tom Wright makes that claim by answering his own question, "Why then did people go on talking about Jesus of Nazareth, except as a remarkable but tragic memory?" by saying that "Jesus was raised from the dead."[29] You yourself, Dale, never make that claim and, as far as I can see, you would not and could not do so. One reason is that, having said that Jesus and all other millenarian prophets were wrong (so far), you could hardly claim that God raised Jesus from the dead to prove he alone was transcendentally wrong. Another, and less facetious reason is this. Resurrection is part and parcel of apocalypticism and stands or falls with it. Wrong on apocalyptic vision, wrong on resurrection faith. Wrong, at least, on what those earliest Christians meant by both of those phenomena. Everything in 1 Corinthians 15 and the gospels' final chapters could still be taken literally (if one wished), but they would be describing Elijah-like *exaltation*, a very special privilege for Jesus himself but not the start of the general *resurrection* and the end of the world. You might, then, for example, still have Phil 2:6–11, but that is sublime *exaltation*, not necessarily apocalyptic *resurrection*. If Jesus' announcement of apocalyptic consummation was wrong, then earliest Christianity's announcement of Jesus' *resurrection* was likewise wrong. Indeed, since resurrection could only intensify apocalyptic expectation (the general resurrection had actually begun!), it could but increase that wrongness. I do not use, in honor of your own honesty, the solution that all of this was not about the imminent first-century but about (at least, and counting) the twenty-first century. In any case, resurrection cannot compensate for being wrong when it itself is included in that wrongness.

29. Wright, *Jesus and the Victory of God*, 658–59.

## (3) Synthesis

I still work within your own thesis but suggest six distinctions within apocalypticism necessary to accept both an apocalyptically inevitable mistake and a successfully expanding mission, that is, adequately to explain what actually happened in earliest Christianity. I do not intend my terms to be in any way tendentious but, if they are, we should rename them and debate the concepts rather than the words.

### Destructive or Transformative Apocalypse

We are in complete and actual agreement on the necessary and very important distinction between divine destruction of the material earth (creation repealed) and divine transformation of the unjust world (evil repulsed). Millenarianists or apocalypticists usually want only the latter event and, even if the former is ever envisaged, it is only as a subordinate part or necessary concomitant to that latter event. In any case, it is that latter event which is primarily or exclusively in focus. (Here I abstract from contemporary apocalyptic nihilism or modern terroristic millenarianism where cosmic destruction may be exactly and exclusively in mind.) Cosmic catastrophe or material cataclysm, no matter how terrible or total, is not the same as millenarian consummation. I agree, therefore, that "most millenarian movements, whether ancient, medieval, or modern, have expected not the utter destruction and replacement of this world but rather a revolutionary change."[30] You conclude, for Jesus, "'Heaven on earth,' we might say."[31] That is, as you know, exactly the same phrase I used for apocalypticism in *The Historical Jesus*: "The everlasting Kingdom is apocalyptic, however, not in the sense of a destroyed earth and an evacuation heavenward for the elect, but rather of something like a heaven on earth."[32] It is, I think, necessary to emphasize this both in current scholarship and in contemporary popularization much more now than ever before. Hollywood's *Armageddon* is not the Bible's Armageddon. Hollywood's *Deep Impact* is not the Bible's divine justice. I do not think that we scholars, even or especially in our debates on an apocalyptic versus a non-apocalyptic Jesus, have insisted enough on that fundamental distinction

---

30. Allison, *Jesus*, 156.
31. Allison, *Jesus*, 156.
32. Crossan, *Historical Jesus*, 285.

between an ending of material earth and an ending of human injustice, between the amorality and secularity of current millenarianism and the morality and divinity of ancient millenarianism. But, granted our agreement on that understanding of millenarian or apocalyptic hope, I want to press you to probe more deeply the lineaments of such revolutionary changes promising a heaven on earth. I propose, therefore, a second distinction, but now within that latter understanding of transformative apocalypse as the elimination of earthly injustice, as the process of bringing the world to its knees before God.

### Material or Social Apocalypse

I fine-focus here on your argument that apocalyptic language is to be taken literally and not metaphorically. (Two asides. One: are you just being therapeutically provocative here? Was Virgil being literal with an imminent golden age not needing dye-works as lambs would be born already hued to purple, saffron, and scarlet? Two: even if that is metaphorical, one must still ask metaphorical of *what*? Is it of imperial peace established by the Roman God of power or of cosmic equality established by the Jewish God of justice?). My point here is not to argue for metaphoricity but, working *within your own argument*, to consider ancient *priorities* in such an allegedly literal totality. I am avoiding a division in apocalyptic language between what is literal and what is metaphorical by asking a different question: within that language, what is necessary, unnegotiable, and essential; what is unnecessary, negotiable, and unessential? My question is not rhetorical but historical, I think I know the answer to it, and I ask if you agree with me. I am raising a very general question about Jewish and/or Christian apocalypticism within cross-cultural millenarianism, but I do so with the Sibylline Oracles 2 as specific case-in-point.

You mention celestial inversions such as darkened sun, shrouded moon, falling stars, and shaken celestial powers. You conclude that, "maybe Mk 13:24 should be taken to mean what it says, just like Sib. Or. 2:200–202."[33] But why would anyone have wanted that celestial inversion-effect in which the unusual arrival of darkness replaced the usual normalcy of light unless it was

---

33. Allison, *Jesus*, 161.

accompanied by a terrestrial inversion-effect in which the unusual arrival of justice replaced the usual normalcy of injustice? Granted, for here and now, that one is neither metaphorical nor metonymical of the other, what about priorities within that double inversion? On the one hand, would it be apocalyptically adequate to get justice without darkness? On the other, would it be apocalyptically adequate to get darkness without justice? If millenarians could not have both, which would they have chosen? What, if one had to choose, was essential, what unessential?

I generalize that question by dividing the apocalyptic scenario into three moments, effects, phenomena, or events. Once again, neither divisions nor terms are intended to be tendentious and may be changed to make the conceptual debate as clear as possible. These are my general categories within an apocalyptic consummation:

**Event A:** Peoples (vengeance and/or justice established, universal peace, total equality, etc.)
**Event B:** Lands (abundant fertility, unlabored husbandry, all animals domesticated, etc.)
**Event C:** Heavens (darkened sun, lightless moon, stars falling, etc.)

Those are only representative and you may want to include other categories, but they are enough to ask my basic question. Granted that millenarians thought of them as one undifferentiated package, try to imagine what they would have to say if confronted with this choice: You can have the social Event A without the material Events BC, or you can have the material Events BC without the social Event A. They would surely have opted for Event A above all others, and that has to do with priority of A even if not the metaphoricity of BC. They wanted Event A but could imagine it only within a totality of Events ABC. Total apocalypse is all those social and material elements, all of Events ABC together. Social apocalypse is Event A as a priority within that totality.

For a specific example, consider your own citation of Sibylline Oracles 2. Event C is certainly there, just as you cited: "the heavenly luminaries will crash together" and "all the stars will fall together from heaven on the sea" (2:200–202). Event B is also there in "life without care," in "three springs of wine, honey, and milk," in an earth that "will then bear more abundant fruits spontaneously," and in a world with "no spring, no summer, no winter, no autumn" (2:316, 318, 321–22, 328). But so also is Event A. After the punishment of the unjust, this is the reward of those who "were concerned with justice and noble deeds" (2:319–20, 321–24):

> The earth will belong equally to all, undivided by walls or fences. . . .
> Lives will be in common and wealth will have no division.
> For there will be no poor man there, no rich, and no tyrant,
> no slave. Further, no one will be either great or small anymore.
> No kings, no leaders. All will be on a par together.

John Collins, whose translation I am gratefully using, notes that "most scholars incline to the opinion that such passages were taken over as part of the Jewish original" into their later Christian adaptation and usage.[34] Here is how that apocalyptic vision concludes (2:330–35):

> To these pious ones imperishable God, the universal ruler, will also
> give another thing. Whenever they ask the imperishable God
> to save men from the raging fire and deathless gnashing
> he will grant it, and he will do this.
> For he will pick them out again from the undying fire
> and set them elsewhere and send them on account of his own people

Collins footnotes that one manuscript family inserted a refutation of that gracious conclusion for which it blamed Origen: "Plainly false. For the fire which tortures the condemned will never cease. Even I would pray that this be so, though I am marked with very great scars of faults, which have need of very great mercy. But let babbling Origen be ashamed of saying that there is a limit to punishment."[35] A Christian scribe rejects the Jewish original.

Be that as it may, my question is again about priority, not metaphoricity. What if ancients (or moderns?) had to make this choice? Which do you want: the no-fences world without the no-stars or the no-stars without the no-fences world? Which do you want: the all-on-a-par world without the abundant-fruits-spontaneously or the abundant-fruits-spontaneously without the all-on-

---

34. Collins, "Sybilline Oracles," 330.
35. Collins, "Sybilline Oracles," 353, note c3.

a-par world? Granted they might like it all as a total package deal, and absent any metaphoricity, were all apocalyptic details on the same level of importance or were there clear priorities in everyone's mind?

I think that must be emphasized even if one argues, as you do, that all apocalypticism is more-or-less equally literal. My counter is that, whether Events BC were metaphors, metonyms, enthusiastic hyperboles, exaggerated emphases, or literal expectations, they were nothing without Event A. But Event A alone and by itself was millennium enough, apocalypse now. Event A is essential, Events BC are optional. My next two distinctions, therefore, focus more acutely on that Event A in terms of the just and righteous as against the unjust and unrighteous.

### Primary or Secondary Apocalypse

This distinction occurred to me in thinking about an article by John Kloppenborg, but he should not be held responsible for my reformulation and may not even agree with its content. He distinguished between *apocalyptic* eschatology and what he termed *symbolic* eschatology. His point was that while "it is difficult to miss the pervasive eschatological tenor" of even the sapiential elements in the Q Gospel, "it is another question whether the term apocalyptic is an accurate characterization for the redeployment of these wisdom materials."[36] In other words "it is important to ask whether the presence of an eschatological horizon justifies the label 'apocalyptic.'"[37] He concluded that the Q Gospel used apocalyptic language "creatively to dramatize the transfiguration of the present: apocalyptic symbols lend their force both negatively, by the subverting of confidence in the everydayness of existence, and positively, by buttressing a vision of rich and empowered existence based on the instruction of Jesus."[38] That instruction (better, for me, that lifestyle) was "Q's advocacy of an ethic characterized by non-violence (Q 6:27–28), refusal to participate in normative means of preserving honor through resort to courts or to retaliation (Q 6:29), and the idealization of poverty (6:20b; 12:33–34; 16:13), detachment (14:26–27), and homelessness (9:57–58; 10:4–10)."[39]

36. Kloppenborg, "Symbolic Eschatology," 291.
37. Kloppenborg, "Symbolic Eschatology," 292.
38. Kloppenborg, "Symbolic Eschatology," 304.
39. Kloppenborg, "Symbolic Eschatology," 305.

I rephrase and generalize Kloppenborg's distinction as follows, with appropriate apologies to its author. *Primary* apocalypticism or millenarianism demands immediate actions or extraordinary ethics because of the expectation of imminent consummation. You must give everything away, cease all family relations, retire to the desert, and wait in prayer and fasting for the coming end. The ethical slogan, in other words, is *interim*, and those ethics may be sensible only as such. You might survive being wrong (one might have learned to like the desert) but your future, granted failure, is very precarious. *Secondary* apocalypticism or millenarianism demands immediate actions or extraordinary ethics because of the permanent character and abiding revelation of God. This is how one should be living and what one should be doing here and now in any case, and apocalyptic imminence is sanction rather than cause. This is what God demands and you better pay attention because the end is near. That is what Kloppenborg sees in the Q Gospel. I also see it there and also in the Didache. I think that Didache 16, whether imminent or distant, whether always expected or quietly postponed, is the sanction rather than the basis for Didache 1–15. The failure of Didache 16 to happen will not necessarily destroy that community because its truth is experienced in the success of its lifestyle in imitation of the *tropoi* of the Lord (Jesus/God). The ethical slogan there is *semper interim*.

Compare the following two general admonitions and focus, for example, on their divergent advice about an unmarried virgin woman. First, as an example of primary apocalypticism, think of Paul's advice (not demand) about marriage in 1 Corinthians 7, an advice perfectly reasonable in terms of the approaching end. Celibacy is better, wiser, more appropriate:

> I wish that all were as I myself am. . . . I think that, in view of the impending crisis, it is well for you [virgins] to remain as you are. . . . the appointed time has grown short; from now on, let even those who have wives be as though they had none. . . . and those who deal with the world as though they had no dealings with it. For the present form of this world is passing away (1 Cor 7:7, 26, 29, 31).

Second, as a counter-example of secondary apocalypticism, think about this demand (not advice) from Qumran's Damascus Document:

> And this is the rule of the Many, to provide for all their needs: the salary of two days each month at least. They shall place it in the hand

of the Inspector and of the judges. From it they shall give to the orphans and with it they shall strengthen the hand of the needy and the poor, and to the elder who [is dy]ing, and to the vagabond, and to the prisoner of a foreign people, and to the girl who has no protector, and to the unma[rried woman] who has no suitor; and for all the works of the company, and [the house of the company shall not be deprived of its means]. (CD-A , col. XIV).

I confess for myself, by the way, that falling stars, laborless fertility, and the panoply of most apocalyptic scenarios are far easier to imagine or expect than to imagine let alone expect a non-violent world (or a non-violent God). That absolutely staggers my imagination. I also confess that *sustained* and non-violent resistance to the cosmic normalcy of structural injustice strikes me as impossible without transcendental sources for such conviction, courage, and continuance.

### Negative or Positive Apocalypse

I also took this distinction from another scholar and, although I am not reformulating or renaming it as I did that preceding one, its author should not be held responsible for my present usage. Paula Fredriksen asked this question: "The twelve tribes are restored, the people gathered back to the Land, the Temple and Jerusalem are renewed and made splendid, the Davidic monarch restored: God's Kingdom is established. What place, if any, do Gentiles have in such a kingdom?" She responds: "We can cluster the material around two poles. At the negative extreme, the nations are destroyed, defeated, or in some way subjected to Israel. . . . At the positive extreme, the nations participate in Israel's redemption. The nations will stream to Jerusalem and worship the God of Jacob together with Israel."[40] Both results are present side-by-side in Micah, for example. The negative pole is in Mic 5:15 as God warns that, "in anger and wrath I will execute vengeance on the nations that did not obey." The positive pole is in Mic 4:1–4.

In days to come the mountain of the Lord's house
    shall be established as the highest of the mountains,
    and shall be raised up above the hills.

40. Fredriksen, "Judaism," 544–45.

Peoples shall stream to it,
    and many nations shall come and say:
"Come, let us go up to the mountain of the Lord,
    to the house of the God of Jacob;
    that he may teach us his ways and that we may walk in his paths."
For out of Zion shall go forth instruction,
    and the word of the Lord from Jerusalem.
He shall judge between many peoples,
    and shall arbitrate between strong nations far away.
They shall beat their swords into plowshares,
    and their spears into pruning hooks;
    nation shall not lift up sword against nation,
    neither shall they learn war any more;
but they shall all sit under their own vines and fig trees
    and no one shall make them afraid;
    for the mouth of the Lord of hosts has spoken.

First, Gentiles are not exterminated because they are Gentiles but because Gentiles had increasingly oppressed Israel ever since she became a colony of successive imperial conquerors. Second, they are not converted to become ethnically Jews, but while remaining Gentiles (for example, males would not be circumcised), they are converted to the justice and righteousness, morality and ethics of the Jewish God. I agree with Fredriksen on that point.

> Eschatological Gentiles, . . . those who would gain admission to the Kingdom once it was established, would enter as Gentiles. They would worship and eat together with Israel, in Jerusalem, at the Temple. The God they worship, the God of Israel, will have redeemed them from the error of idolatry: he will have saved them − to phrase this in slightly different idiom − graciously, apart from the works of the Law.[41]

Third, Fredriksen considers that choice of a positive-inclusive solution (conversion) as against a negative-exclusive one (extermination) for the problem of Gentile oppressors at God's apocalyptic consummation "a prominent (indeed predominant) strain of Jewish apocalyptic expectation"[42] and concludes that "it is the inclusive tradition anticipating gentile participation in Israel's final redemption that sounds increasingly in intertestamental writ-

41. Fredriksen, "Judaism," 548.
42. Fredriksen, "Judaism," 553.

ings, in later synagogue prayers, and in rabbinic discussion."[43] (I would like that to be a correct conclusion but am not sure about it). Fourth, Fredriksen also maintains that it was conversion rather than extermination which was accepted in earliest Christian Judaism: "The original apostles would have readily accepted these Gentiles, because such a response was consonant with a . . . strain of Jewish apocalyptic expectation with which the earliest movement — also Jewish also apocalyptic — aligned itself."[44] Or again: "It is the inclusive tradition anticipating gentile participation in Israel's final redemption that. . . . is the tradition shaping the convictions and activities of the earliest Jewish Christians — James, John, Peter, Barnabas, and most especially Paul (see Gal 2)."[45] (I leave aside for now whether that was true for all or only some of those earliest Christian Jews.)

That choice between, in Fredriksen's terms, negative or positive extremes, is also, in my terms, the choice between human extermination or human conversion, between divine vengeance or divine justice and, ultimately, between transcendental violence or transcendental non-violence. It is a question whether God's final solution to evil is the genocidal slaughter of all evil-doers. It is a question about transcendental eth(n)ic cleansing. It is a question for both Jews and Christians. I think you agreed with her (and me) on that final suggestion when you said that, "the existence of an early mission to Gentiles strongly suggests that he [Jesus] didn't anticipate their eschatological annihilation." But if Jewish Christians accepted apocalyptic Gentile inclusivity, there was one subsequent decision they had to make then, and one consequent distinction we have to make now.

### Passive or Active Apocalypse

When those earliest Christian Jews accepted conversion rather than extermination as God's apocalyptic scenario for the pagans, and even when (to be seen below) they accepted Jesus' resurrection as the start of that scenario's finale, they were still faced by one more major problem. Should we wait in prayer and holiness for those pagans to be brought to Zion's eschatological banquet by the power of God? Or should we go out on missionary jour-

43. Fredriksen, *Jesus*, 129.
44. Fredriksen, "Judaism," 553.
45. Fredriksen, *Jesus*, 129.

neys to bring them in? Is it about God without us or about us with God? That is what I mean by passive or active apocalypticsm and I acknowledge that "passive" may not be the best word to describe expectant lives of purity, prayer, holiness, and hope. But this is the basic distinction. Is apocalypticism about human hope and expectation for a divine action, a transcendental solution to the problem of evil, injustice, and violence? Or is it about anything we should do in time, place, and history to participate in that process? Or, is it about both together? Is it about passive expectation or active cooperation?

We know that missionary activity among pagans started very early and that it did not demand male circumcision. We know it was accepted even by James of Jerusalem. It was there before Paul, was what led him to persecute Christian Jews in Damascus, and was that to which he was later both converted and called. Thereafter, it was certainly a major characteristic of pauline theology (but not of the Q Gospel?). Furthermore, were some of those who opposed Paul not so much "Judaizers" (a terribly inappropriate term, in any case) but Christian Jews who thought that the conversion of the Gentiles was, even or especially *within* their apocalyptic scenario, an affair to be left up to God alone?

It was utterly possible and probably inevitable that some Christian Jews could accept that entire apocalyptic scenario and still conclude that their function was to live in holiness and fidelity, prayer and expectation, and for God alone to flood Jerusalem with apocalyptically converted Gentiles. But we know for certain that at least some of them drew the opposite conclusion. Their extensive missionary activity indicated not just an expectant (we are waiting for God), but a cooperative (God is waiting for us) apocalypticism.

I reject utterly any interpretation of what I have just said as meaning that it is all up to us and that the mention of "God" is simply polite window-dressing. I reject, therefore, your "attempt to resist correlating Jesus' eschatological vision with anything history has had to offer" since apocalyptic eschatology "is a transcendent and universal solution to the problem of evil."[46] I reject it both for them then and for myself now. I think their intense missionary activity came from people who believed in "incarnation" and concluded that an incarnational apocalypse meant active

---

46. Below, pp. 100-101.

cooperation and not just passive expectation. Why else did Paul not stay at home, mind his own business, and leave that apocalyptic conversion of the Gentiles up to a universality beyond historical action and a transcendence beyond human cooperation? Neither God without Paul, then, nor Paul without God.

### Instantive or Durative Apocalypse

I find it difficult to keep this distinction separate from the preceding one, but here goes. I refer to a distinction within one's understanding of apocalyptic *consummation*, within one's vision of the great apocalyptic *finale*. I know, of course, that apocalypse was always seen as a durative phenomenon. There would be sufferings and disasters, wars and rumors of wars, signs and portents as the consummation approached. But a climactic moment such as the general resurrection was instantive rather than durative, immediate rather than prolonged.

I noted above that, "Resurrection is part and parcel of apocalypticism and stands or falls with it. Wrong on apocalyptic vision, wrong on resurrection faith. Wrong, at least, on what those earliest Christians meant by both of those phenomena."[47] Here I emphasize its significance in this entire debate. If we can say that those early Christian Jews were wrong about apocalypse, then they were also wrong about Jesus' resurrection. Yet those who confessed that resurrection, continued to do so just as forcibly as ever across that first century. (And non-apocalyptic Christians still do to this day).

The general resurrection was the climax of the apocalyptic scenario, and if that scenario was itself a duration, that climax was supposed to be an instant, a conclusion, a grand finale. Thus, as Sibylline Oracles 2:226 put it, "bodies of humans, made solid in heavenly manner, breathing and set in motion, will be raised on a single day." That is what I mean by the general resurrection as instantive apocalyptic consummation. A single day is instantive, two thousand years are durative. But certain early Christian Jews said something completely new, creatively new, uniquely new.

I pause here for a warning. I emphatically do not speak of any uniqueness of Christianity over against Judaism, but of a unique option within Judaism itself. For example, a general apocalyptic hope could have or not have a messianic protagonist. If present,

47. Above, p. 55.

he could be angelic or human. If human, he could be king, prophet, or priest. Thus, for instance, Essene Jews could uniquely invent the single coming of a double Messiah (priest and king, separate, in that order, and presumably anti-Hasmonean). Similarly, Christian Jews could uniquely invent the double coming of a single Messiah (in the past with suffering and execution, in the future with glory and triumph). Those were unique creations within and not against Judaism. Similarly here with apocalyptic consummation seen not as instantive but durative. It was not Christianity against Judaism, but it was (certain segments of ?) Christian Judaism against other segments of Judaism (and even of Christian Judaism?).

Those Christian Jews who opted for a durative apocalyptic consummation did not assert the future-imminence of apocalypse, but rather its past-advent. It was not just coming soon, it had already begun. In fact, the climactic element was span rather than moment. I take that primarily from Paul in I Corinthians 15. Jesus' resurrection was not a matter of personal exaltation (like Enoch or Elijah), but was the start of the general resurrection itself, the beginning of the apocalyptic climax. That shows, implicitly, how Paul can reverse the argument in 1 Cor 15:12–13: no Jesus-resurrection, no general-resurrection; no general-resurrection, no Jesus-resurrection. It shows, explicitly, in 1 Cor 15:20 where "Christ has been raised from the dead, the first fruits of those who have died." With first-fruits, the harvest is no longer imminent but has actually begun. Paul certainly thought that the duration between start and end would be short and there he was quite wrong. But if Christians then or now believe in Jesus' resurrection, they/we are asserting that apocalypse is duration not instant, and that it has already begun. They/we, then, had better be able to show how their/our communities have introduced islands of non-violent justice in a world of violent injustice. It is always safe to proclaim an imminent apocalypse because, as you noted, Dale, it has so far always been wrong. But that is not what those Christian Jews represented, for example, by 1 Cor 15, were asserting. They claimed it was already present, although not finished of course, and I think Paul would have been quite ready to bring interested pagans into his communities, into the share-meals known as the Lord's (style of) Supper, and into miniature worlds of non-violent justice. And to say: see for yourself.

It all comes down to this: We regularly quote or have quoted against us this saying of Paul from 1 Cor 15:14 that, "if Christ has not been raised, then our proclamation has been in vain and your faith has been in vain." True, of course. But, then, so is its reversal. If our faith has been in vain (that is, if it is not visibly and publicly making the world more divinely just), then Christian proclamation has been in vain (that is, if it is not about making the world more divinely just), and Christ has not been raised (that is, as the *start* of the general resurrection and apocalyptic consummation). Exalted, maybe (as in Psalm 2), but certainly not raised.

### (4) Conclusion

Dale, you interpret Jesus and earliest Christianity in apocalyptic continuity within the matrix of millenarian expectation or eschatological hope. You say that, like all such, they were not only "wrong"[48] but "essentially irrational."[49] Granted that position, you must explain why, even within the period of that irrational error, their message and mission did not slowly decline and steadily disappear. If I may use your own somewhat unfortunate juridical expression, my "case against" Dale Allison is, once again, this: why did longer and wronger get stronger and stronger? (If we are in court, why not Cochrane-style?) My suggestion, working within your own thesis, postulates the necessity of qualifying their eschatological/apocalyptic/millenarian expectation not only as transformative rather than destructive (we agree there), but also as social rather than material, as secondary rather than primary, as positive rather than negative, as active rather than passive, and as durative rather than instantive in resurrectional finale. There are fleeting, all too fleeting, hints of some of those distinctions in your text. For example, you ask: "Did [Jesus] live with the expectation that not just dispersed Israel but righteous Gentiles would go up to Zion" but you decline "to fill out the details of Jesus' eschatological vision."[50] But, Dale, God is in the details. Or again, but only in a footnote, you note that "Jesus seems to have muted the element of vengeance in his eschatological language."[51] I find that terribly weak, especially in terms of, first, your proposed

---

48. Allison, *Jesus*, 218.
49. Allison, *Jesus*, 4.
50. Allison, *Jesus*, 152.
51. Allison, *Jesus*, 171, note 285.

apocalyptic continuity, and, second, the earliest and pre-Pauline acceptance of Gentile converts.

It is necessary, I suggest, to desimplify the current easy confrontation of "apocalyptic" versus "non-apocalyptic" Jesus and to admit that there are complicating positions from scholars (for example, Koester, Kloppenborg, Patterson, and myself, to name just a few), who envisage an eschatological but non-apocalyptic Jesus. In my own case, for instance, an "apocalyptic" Jesus and/or earliest Christianity where the emphasis is on transformative, social, secondary, positive, active, and durative apocalyptic rather than on destructive, material, primary, negative, passive, and instantive apocalyptic, is so close to what I have termed ethical eschatology or the radicality of divine ethics,[52] that I am not certain what would still be worth a continuing argument. Maybe, I shall find out! But what makes *such* an "apocalyptic" Jesus persuasive is not that it agrees with me but that it explains what actually happened to the Kingdom movement across its first hundred years.

## STEPHEN PATTERSON

In 1990 James M. Robinson, addressing the International Society of Biblical Literature, assessed the state of historical Jesus research 30 years after the appearance of his watershed chronicle of *The New Quest of the Historical Jesus.* Among his observations perhaps none were more significant and controversial than those having to do with eschatology. Robinson declared that nothing less than a revolution had taken place in the way scholars had come to view Jesus. It can no longer be assumed, he said, that the preaching of Jesus was characterized by intense apocalyptic expectation. Robinson's remarks came after a decade of rejuvenated historical interest in Jesus, a development brought about in no small measure by the work of the Jesus Seminar, founded in 1985 by Robert W. Funk. For support, he could point to surveys by Marcus Borg of the SBL Historical Jesus Section and of the Jesus Seminar itself, which indicated that a majority of scholars active in these two groups had in fact abandoned the century-old consensus, made popular by Albert Schweitzer, that Jesus was an apocalyptic

---

52. See *The Birth of Christianity,* 273–89.

prophet. Such shifts do not come easily. Indeed, the lively, if sometimes acrimonious, discussion of this matter that has unfolded in the last decade indicates that not everyone is ready yet to abandon Schweitzer's view. If the 1980s saw a revolution in the way we view Jesus, the 1990s have brought on the counter-revolution, of which Dale Allison's book is perhaps the best example.

In a 1995 essay[53] I listed the developments in scholarship that, in my estimation, had brought about the collapse of the consensus that so long attended Schweitzer's view. This is where I shall begin.

## The Collapse of the Apocalyptic Consensus

The undermining of Schweitzer's apocalyptic understanding of Jesus had been brewing for a long time. It began, in fact, with the work of some of the New Questers in the 1950s. Hans Conzelmann[54] and Ernst Käsemann,[55] for example, doubted that Jesus entertained the same future-oriented, apocalyptic expectations as had John the Baptist. His message, rather, focused on an immediate reign of God that he associated with his own person and preaching. Käsemann summarizes:

> The fact of the matter is surely that while Jesus did take his start from the apocalyptically determined message of John the Baptist, yet his own preaching was not constitutively stamped by apocalyptic but proclaimed the immediate nearness of God. I am convinced that the man who took this step cannot have awaited the coming Son of Man, the restoration of the twelve tribes in the messianic kingdom, and therewith the dawn of the *parousia*, as the means of experiencing the nearness of God.[56]

Käsemann's contemporary, Philipp Vielhauer, came to similar conclusions through his research on the origin of the synoptic Son of Man sayings.[57] Vielhauer's tradition-historical work showed that all of these sayings (save one, Matt 24:37–39: here the matter

53. Patterson, "The End of Apocalypse."
54. Conzelmann, "Present and Future."
55. Käsemann, "Beginnings."
56. Käsemann, "Beginnings," 39–40.
57. Vielhauer, "Gottesreich und Menschensohn".

remains undecided) are products of later Christian tradition. This confirmed what he had suspected from his survey of early Jewish literature, where he found that the Son of Man figure and the idea of God reigning on earth do not really belong together. The former belongs to future-oriented apocalyptic speculation, the latter to the present hope of God reigning now. Vielhauer concluded that the future-oriented, apocalyptic Son of Man sayings were fundamentally incompatible with Jesus' proclamation of the reign of God. Thus, one of the basic issues in today's debate had already emerged in the 1950s: did Jesus carry John the Baptist's apocalyptic ideas with him into his own message, or was Jesus' notion of the reign of God as already present one of the points which separated him from John? Many New Questers held the latter view.

The apocalyptic hypothesis was further undermined along these same lines amidst the revitalized discussion of Jesus' parables in the 1960s. Schweitzer would have read the parables as he found them in Mark and Matthew as allegories for the future judgment, and assumed that Jesus had created them with this in mind. But this reading of the parables had already been blocked by Adolf Jülicher's monumental work at the turn of the century, which had shown the allegorization of Jesus' parables to be secondary.[58] If they were not originally allegories, then what were the parables? The way scholars are apt to answer this question today was shaped in large measure by the work of a group of scholars — including Crossan and Funk — under the leadership of Amos Wilder, who labored in the Parables Seminar of the Society of Biblical Literature in the 1960s and 70s. Wilder argued that the parables are narrative metaphors — that is, stories through which the world of God's kingdom might come to life in the imagination of the listener. This idea, now widely accepted, was related to the New Questers' idea that Jesus spoke not of a future, apocalyptic event, but of the immediate reign of God, now present in the potential of the human imagination to see the world differently and to act accordingly. Given the central role still played by the parables in most scholars' reconstruction of Jesus' preaching, this development, perhaps more than any other, prepared scholars to re-evaluate the part played by apocalypticism in Jesus' message.

Two more recent developments have been particularly instrumental in bringing about the turn away from apocalyptic. The

58. Jülicher, *Die Gleichnisreden Jesu.*

first has to do with Q, that collection of sayings used by Matthew and Luke. Over the past thirty years, Q has been the object of intense study, leading to the reconstruction of its basic content, and some understanding of how this document came to be. In the 1960s and 70s studies appeared[59] which showed that whoever gave Q its final form had a strongly apocalyptic agenda. In 1987 John Kloppenborg published his very influential study of Q,[60] which confirmed this basic hypothesis. Kloppenborg used literary analysis to isolate those final, shaping apocalyptic touches in reconstructed Q passages. But Kloppenborg's analysis turned up something else as well. Beneath this final layer of apocalyptic judgment, there is embedded in Q a series of speeches which exhibit their own coherence of style and content. They are made up, for the most part, of wisdom sayings in various forms: aphorisms, beatitudes, and parables. Kloppenborg concluded that this series of wisdom speeches attributed to Jesus comprised the first edition of Q, He called this first edition $Q^1$, the later apocalyptic layer $Q^2$.

Kloppenborg's work gave concrete evidence for what Helmut Koester had been arguing for several years based upon another early Christian sayings collection, the Gospel of Thomas. The integration of this second early Christian sayings gospel into the discussion of Christian origins is another more recent development that has undermined the apocalyptic hypothesis. The Gospel of Thomas is important because, while it shares many of the sayings found in the synoptic tradition, its author appears not to have made use of the synoptic gospels themselves. Thus, it gives scholars an independent source for many sayings of Jesus known previously only through the synoptic gospels, and consequently another lens through which to study the development of the sayings tradition. What Koester noticed in Thomas was the absence of the apocalypticism so characteristic of these sayings in the synoptic tradition. He speculated that the Thomas tradition was derived from a stage in the development of the sayings tradition that pre-dated the appearance of the Son of Man apocalypticism found in Q.[61]

---

59. Lührmann, *Die Redaktion der Logienquelle*; Jacobson, *Wisdom Christology in Q*, later expanded in *The First Gospel*.
60. Kloppenborg, *Formation of Q*.
61. Koester, "One Jesus."

Kloppenborg's work on Q demonstrated that, at least in the development of the Q tradition, there was indeed such a pre-apocalyptic stage. In my own work on the Gospel of Thomas I sought to fill in this picture of the early sayings tradition further.[62] If Thomas is indeed an independent witness to the development of the sayings tradition, then a comparison of parallel sayings in Thomas and the synoptic gospels should tell us something about the development of this tradition. Those elements shared by Thomas and the synoptic tradition will have had their origin, one might conclude, early on in its formation, while those that appear only in one or the other will have had their origin relatively late. What I found in comparing Q and Thomas was that both texts contained a basic corpus of wisdom sayings associated with Jesus. This, I concluded, must derive from a very early stage in the development of the sayings tradition. The apocalypticism of Q was not found in Thomas, but only in Q. This, I assumed, must have arisen in the Q tradition (or perhaps more generally, in the synoptic tradition, since Mark also shares it). For its part, neither had Thomas preserved all of its sayings of Jesus in a pristine, unaltered sapiential form. Many sayings in the Thomas tradition had been shaped by the more speculative and esoteric forms of Jewish Wisdom theology, even Gnosticism. Q shared little of this. I therefore concluded that, like Q's apocalypticism, the esoteric and Gnostic tendencies of the Thomas tradition belonged not to the early stages of the sayings tradition, but to a later period, when the tradition had begun to develop in diverse ways. Similar results would obtain for comparisons between Thomas and Mark, or Thomas and the special traditions associated with either Matthew or Luke.

All of this suggests that Jesus' sayings were originally collected by followers who were interested in him as a wisdom teacher, or perhaps as Lady Wisdom's prophet, a figure common in Jewish Wisdom theology. Later, people associated with the development of the synoptic tradition began to interpret Jesus' message in light of Jewish apocalyptic theology. On the other hand, people associated with the Thomas tradition began to see him as a revealer of secret and hidden wisdom, one of the core elements in Gnosticism. More than a prophet, he was the descending/ascending savior sent by God to enlighten humanity.

62. Patterson, "Wisdom in Q and Thomas."

What seemed compelling to me about this picture was the way in which it might be reflected elsewhere in early Christianity as well. The Gospel of John, which depicts Jesus not as an apocalyptic figure, but a savior sent from God to enlighten the world, now no longer seemed to appear from out of nowhere. In fact, Koester was able to show how John's long, mysterious discourses might have developed out of early collections of sayings similar to those found in Thomas.[63] On the other hand, it helped to explain aspects of Pauline Christianity as well. Paul himself has never been a mystery: his apocalypticism seemed to be in step with what we knew of the rest of early Christianity. But his opponents, whose ideas must be divined obliquely through the arguments Paul offers to rebut them, have always been very mysterious. But now some of them seem not quite so inexplicable. His First Corinthian opponents, for example, would have been quite at home with a Thomas-like understanding of the Jesus tradition. They, too, were interested in Jesus as a revealer of secret and hidden wisdom.

These studies on Q, Thomas, and the development of the sayings tradition have an indirect yet significant bearing on historical Jesus research. For since Schweitzer it has been assumed that the synoptic presentation of Jesus' preaching is the earliest and most reliable evidence we have for determining the nature of his message. The apocalypticism of Q and Mark (corroborated by Paul) seemed to indicate beyond a reasonable doubt that Jesus was an apocalyptic prophet. Now, however, it appears that the apocalypticism of the synoptic tradition was built upon an earlier wisdom foundation, much of which can still be recovered through critical analysis. As the followers of Jesus reflected on his significance in the years following his death, at least two streams of thought quickly developed: one that came to understand him in terms of Jewish apocalypticism, and another that saw him rather in terms of the more esoteric forms of Jewish wisdom theology and eventually Gnosticism. The most logical inference from this is that Jesus presented himself neither as an apocalyptic prophet, nor as a Gnostic revealer sent from God. He was seen, rather, as a teacher of wisdom, or perhaps one of Wisdom's prophets.

---

63. Koester, "Dialog und Spruchüberlieferung;" "Gnostic Sayings;" *Ancient Christian Gospels*, 256–67.

## Comments on Dale's Response

Dale is not convinced that the studies discussed above have in fact undermined the apocalyptic hypothesis. Indeed, they have had little impact on his view at all. Let us begin with the older work.

Dale dismisses the views of Käsemann, Conzelmann, and Vielhauer in a brief paragraph, sending us back to an earlier discussion on the problem of the authenticity of the Son of Man sayings. "Any claim here is precarious," he warns, since the matter remains unsettled.[64] Perhaps so. But while Vielhauer chose to focus his work around the Son of Man issue, this was not really the point of what the New Questers were seeing. What interested them was the tension between the future-oriented apocalypticism of, say Mark 13, and the present orientation of such sayings as Luke 17:20–21:

> The kingdom of God is not coming with things that can be observed; nor will they say, "Look, here it is!" or "There it is!" For, in fact, the kingdom of God is among you.

Was the person who said this the same person who carefully enumerated the signs of the coming of the Son of Man in Mark 13? The New Questers did not think so.

Dale's approach to the parables discussion is similarly brief and dismissive. Parables, he argues, are most notoriously multivalent: they are what one will make of them. Jesus might have meant them to be heard as apocalyptic code language, or he might not have. We just do not know. Allison concludes, "that this debate will be decided by what we make of the parables seems most doubtful."[65]

But we know more than Allison will admit here. It is seldom disputed, for example, that the highly coded, esoteric language of allegorical interpretation was not originally part of Jesus' parables. On the contrary, their multivalency derives in part from their open, inviting quality, their use of familiar scenes and clear scenarios, such that anyone can understand what is happening and experience the story for himself or herself. The allegorization of the parables was the church's way of limiting this multiplicity of

64. Allison, *Jesus*, 128.
65. Allison, *Jesus*, 128.

meaning by fixing it on a single imagined, unfolding apocalyptic scenario. Now, if the apocalyptic understanding of the parables was bound up with their secondary allegorization, it only stands to reason that this apocalyptic interpretation itself was also late. Without it, there is no reason to read apocalypticism into the parables. Indeed, the open, multivalent quality of Jesus' parables stands in stark contrast to the typically closed, fixed quality of apocalyptic. The whole point of apocalyptic literature is to reveal to initiates the secret of how exactly the end will unfold. In other words, one cannot embrace the current understanding of Jesus' parables as open, multivalent language events (as Dale seems to do), while at the same time clinging to an apocalyptic understanding of them.

The question of Jesus' parables is much too important to leave out of this debate. How we understand them will impact dramatically how we understand that central concept in Jesus' preaching, the reign of God. A good many of the parables, after all, begin in just this way: the reign of God is like. . . . When we remove from the parables the late, allegorical, apocalyptically charged editorial work of the evangelists, there is little in the tradition that would cause one to think that Jesus associated the reign of God with an apocalyptic event at all. And this is just what we should expect on the basis of Vielhauer's work, and later that of Mack and Crossan, who have pointed out that the term "reign of God" is not to be found in the apocalyptic literature of ancient Judaism. It belongs rather to the discourse of wisdom theology, and the question of what constitutes wise and just rule. Is it any wonder, then, that the most intensely apocalyptic passages in the synoptic gospels (Mark 13, Q 17, and their parallels) do not mention the reign of God? Future-oriented apocalypticism, with its esotericism, and its desire to see the end exactly as it will be, simply does not fit well with the open, more public discourse of wisdom, and its characteristic form, the parable.

And what about the more recent developments in the study of Q and the Gospel of Thomas? Dale is also unimpressed with their results, and so is not yet ready to incorporate them into his view.

First, Dale is generally skeptical, as many are, of Q research. How far can one proceed in the study of a document that is lost, and must therefore first be reconstructed? Thus, he concludes that Kloppenborg's work is simply not yet the firm result of thoroughly tested scholarship. But even if one were to accept Kloppenborg's work, there are, he argues, apocalyptic sayings in Kloppenborg's early, $Q^1$ layer. Finally, if most of the apocalypticism of Q comes in $Q^2$, must we therefore conclude that $Q^1$'s sapiential orientation is closer to Jesus' preaching? Why not assume that $Q^1$ was tendentious, and that $Q^2$, whose apocalypticism is consistent with Paul and Mark, corrects the errors of $Q^1$ by adding apocalyptic back into the tradition?

There is no answer, of course, to generalized skepticism, so I will lay aside Dale's first point for now; later I will say more about Dale's general mistrust of historical critical work as the basis for historical Jesus research. His second point, that there is apocalyptic in $Q^1$, is credited to Helmut Koester. But Dale here misunderstands Koester, who indeed thinks of Jesus as an eschatological prophet in "the most original version of Q," but "eschatological" in the general utopian sense of this word, not necessarily apocalyptic. The beatitudes in Q 6:20–23, the example Dale cites, Koester and others regard as prophetic and utopian, but not apocalyptic. This utopian strain in wisdom literature, its tendency to speak in ideal terms, perhaps explains how wisdom can so easily give way to apocalypticism when those ideals are not realized. But the beatitude itself is a wisdom form, not an apocalyptic form.

As for the possibility that $Q^2$ lies closer to Jesus' actual preaching than $Q^1$, one might say that anything is, in theory, *possible*. But is this more *probable* than the reverse? Certainly $Q^2$'s agreement with Paul and Mark on this point does not make it so. Mark is late, and stands in the synoptic stream that was at least indirectly influenced by $Q^2$. Mark provides no independent "take" on the preaching of Jesus. And Paul shows us that an apocalyptic understanding of Jesus had emerged at least as early as Paul's first letter (1 Thessalonians, around 50 C.E.), but the appearance of his Corinthian opponents at about the same time demonstrates that an esoteric, quasi-Gnostic interpretation of Jesus had also emerged by then. Which came first? We do not know. The question must be, then, what shall we posit at the beginning of this diversity of interpretation of Jesus' message that will, most plausibly, account for its complexity?

This brings us to the Gospel of Thomas. One of the key points of dispute about Thomas is whether, and to what extent, it in fact gives us an independent view of the sayings tradition. A generation ago many assumed that the writer of this gospel drew its material from the synoptic gospels, and so presented not an independent view, but a late, derivative, and tendentious view of the tradition. Some still hold this position today, but most recent studies of Thomas have corroborated either its autonomy, or at least the possibility that some of its sayings are independent of the synoptic tradition. Dale does not dispute this, so I assume that we are operating with the same basic critical assumptions about this gospel. But what does it tell us about Jesus and the development of the Jesus tradition? On this we are not in agreement.

Dale believes that the absence of apocalyptic in Thomas is accounted for by the fact that this gospel shows a bias against apocalyptic, and so, presumably, its author edited it out. This is possible in theory, but in reality the evidence does not suggest it. Let us begin with the sayings common to Q and Thomas. Many of these sayings are aphoristic, and so receive their meaning from their interpretive context. In an apocalyptic context they might be read in apocalyptic terms; in a Gnostic context they might be read esoterically. With such sayings, which comprise the vast majority of Q-Thomas parallels, no tendentious editorial work is detectable at all. Where editorial work is clearly present in Thomas, the effect is not to block apocalyptic speculation, but to fuel an esoteric interpretation. On occasion, the alterations one finds in Thomas would be quite compatible with an apocalyptic interpretation if the overall context of the document were to suggest it. For example, in the following instance Thomas adds material to the simple wisdom exhortation to seek after insight:

> Jesus says, "Seek and you will find. But the things you asked me about in past times, and what I did not tell you in that day, now I am willing to tell you, but you do not seek them" (Thom 92).

Notice the content of the second sentence – the redactional part of the saying. It speaks of Jesus' desire to reveal secrets to his followers, a theme equally at home in both apocalyptic and Gnosticism. Now we know from the Thomas context that those secrets do not have to do with the end of the world, but with the nature of the cosmos and with the true essence of human nature. But in adding these words, the editor of Thomas' sayings certainly was not thinking about how to undo an apocalyptic understanding of them.

The situation becomes even clearer when one looks at the parables shared by Thomas and the synoptic tradition. Here the parallels extend throughout the synoptic layers – Q, Mark, Special Matthew, Special Luke. As I have indicated above, it is widely agreed that the allegorical interpretation of the parables found in the synoptic tradition is secondary; moreover, it is precisely through this process of allegorization that certain parables came to be read as predictions of the future judgment. When one looks at the parables in Thomas one finds that without exception they not only lack the apocalyptic turn one finds in their synoptic parallels, they also lack any of the allegorical features by which the apocalyptic reading was achieved. Indeed, the Thomas parables, from a form critical point of view, are generally more primitive than their synoptic counterparts, or derived from versions that were themselves more primitive. Not that the parables in Thomas are preserved in their pristine original form, but where secondary features are evident, they neither build upon, nor explicitly "undo" the editorial work found in the various synoptic gospels. How shall we account for this? It is in theory possible that the editor of the Gospel of Thomas worked diligently and consistently at undoing the work of the synoptic tradition, turning back the tradition-historical clock with utter perfection, only then to add his own touches here and there to spin the parables in a more esoteric direction. But I do not consider this a likely scenario. To me it is infinitely more plausible to posit an early corpus of parables – a common wisdom form – at the heart of Jesus' preaching. Over time, those notoriously multivalent and pliant parables were retold in ways that reflected the unfolding theological interests of various early Christian communities.

## Why Do We Disagree?

As I look over Dale's arguments, as well as his general approach to the problem, I find that there are two fundamental, and intertwined, areas of disagreement between us. The first is perhaps obvious from the above review of Dale's objections to my case: Dale is skeptical of those recent results of historical-critical research that I find to be convincing. More generally, however, Dale does not believe that historical criticism can provide a firm foundation upon which to proceed with the historical Jesus question. Instead, he believes that more general observations about the culture and the gospel tradition give us a better starting point for this work.[66] In my own work I choose to begin with historical criticism as the fundamental basis of all historical research.

The second area of disagreement is related. Dale generally embraces the view that the synoptic gospels represent a main-stream of tradition about Jesus that is basically accurate. Various other traditions branch off and depart from this more authentically preserved voice. In fact, Dale argues, if we cannot trust this synoptic voice, then we must give up all hope of ever recovering something of the historical Jesus.[67] By contrast, I am convinced that the last thirty years of historical critical research on the synoptic tradition, Q, Thomas, the opponents of Paul – Christian origins, generally speaking – suggests a less homogeneous picture. Christianity was a diverse phenomenon from the very beginning; there is no mainstream. The synoptic tradition stands alongside others: Johannine Christianity, Thomasine Christianity, pre-Pauline Hellenistic Jewish Christianity, Palestinian Jewish Christianity, etc., each of which may be glimpsed from the sources. But embracing this view means approaching the quest for the historical Jesus in a different way. The decisive issue is not who preserves the voice of Jesus most reliably, but what sort of message and ministry we can posit at the beginning of this diversity that will plausibly account for it.

In an admirably candid moment, an "Unscientific Postscript," Dale reveals what I believe is the crux of the matter between us. He writes:

> Most of us, after years of studying the Synoptics and their relatives, somehow feel that we have come not just to know a collection of facts about another human being but rather have come to know Jesus in a sense somehow analogous to the way in which we know the people around us: we have formed an idea of the sort of person he must have been. Our unarticulated convictions in this matter have a lot to do with how we go about our business as historians of Jesus.[68]

Dale is, of course, right: the subjective judgments of historians always play a crucial role in the writing of history. But what is striking to me about this statement is the presumed centrality of the synoptic view: however our individual sensibilities might lead

66. Allison, *Jesus*, 30–33, and especially 33–39.
67. Allison, *Jesus*, 34–35.
68. Allison, *Jesus*, 76.

us to see Jesus in different ways, we all start with the synoptic view. *This* is not so much a subjective judgment as an uncritical assumption. It is an assumption I probably would have shared a dozen years ago, when I first joined colleagues around the tables of the Jesus Seminar. But while I worked in this open forum of scholars, one of the first things I discovered was that I could not get away with my uncritical assumptions. Subjective judgments also become a pretty hard sell under that sort of critical scrutiny. My own views about how to understand the tradition, and consequently, how to imagine the historical figure who stood at its beginning, were shaped in that forum. It is hard to dismiss Kloppenborg's work on Q when he is sitting there next to you presenting an exceedingly plausible explanation for what you are seeing in the text. It is difficult to overlook the significance of the parables when Bernard Brandon Scott (*Hear, Then, the Parable*) is across the table from you forcing the issue. For my part, I think that I was able to change a number of minds on the Gospel of Thomas, but I had to do so strictly without any sort of personal privilege.

As I read the ever expanding corpus of secondary literature on Jesus I am struck by the extent to which scholars wish to claim personal privilege on this issue. This is, I believe, one reason why so many scholars have felt the need to distance themselves from the work of the Jesus Seminar. Because this was a *group* of scholars, it was easily assumed that it spoke for "scholars" in general (though the Jesus Seminar did not make this claim). This was an intrusion into sacred personal space. In the "backlash" literature aimed against the Seminar this embattled sense is often palpable, if not explicitly stated. To counter the fact that the Seminar was a *group* of scholars, many spoke of the group as though it were one voice, not many. Dale does this when he attributes to the Seminar a kind of unconscious decision making – what Cardinal Newman called in his *Grammar of Assent* the "illative sense," using factors "too fine to avail separately, too subtle and circuitous to be convertible into syllogisms, too numerous and various for such conversion, even if they were convertible"[69] But a group does not have an "illative sense." And if one wishes to persuade others in an open forum, one's illative sense is of no use at all. To persuade others one must formulate arguments, and be willing to have

69. Allison, *Jesus*, 76, quoting Newman.

them scrutinized by others. A decade of give and take around these issues with peers has made a great deal of difference to me, and to my view of Jesus. The historical critical arguments have meant something to me: they have changed my views over time. I cannot dismiss them or deny their importance. The big picture for me now emerges from the details, from slogging through the muck of historical critical scholarship alongside colleagues who forced me to take their arguments seriously.

I cannot make out the voice of Jesus from general observations on the ancient world, or from the general, homogeneous impression left by the synoptic gospels. For me, the distinctive voice of Jesus has begun to emerge from the careful critical analysis of the sources, from exegesis, from the problems and solutions suggested by the details of the texts themselves. Dale argues that the quest cannot begin here. I am convinced that it must begin here: historical questions can be answered only by historical critical analysis.

# A Response

Dale Allison

"It chanced that, even when he erred the truth was discovered."
– Dr. Watson

I am truly flattered that three prominent historians of Jesus have been moved to respond to my modest book. Of course, the flattery is considerably tempered by the fact that they are persuaded by very little of what I've argued. Sadly, the same is true for me. As this chapter shows, I'm not flying the flag of surrender. I suppose one might have anticipated such mutual obstinacy, yet the situation is discouraging. Presumably some of us have better arguments while others of us have inferior arguments, and the latter think they are the former. I guess all of us are going to die thinking that we know best about the historical Jesus.

One might then put faith in the onlookers to this debate and trust that they will judge who is the more persuasive and so, one hopes, closer to the truth. Yet I expect that they too, whether in the guild or without, will also come to more than one conclusion. My own sense of the situation is that the old days, when one could hope for and work toward a broad consensus on some important issues of scholarship, are well-nigh defunct. Modernity has done to our field what it has done to so many others – it has absconded with the consensus. The historical Jesus is now the captive of pluralism and diversity. I suspect that the debate over his eschatology, which has already been with us for over a century, is not going away anytime soon. Perhaps the best that we can hope for, then, is to clarify some of the issues, and that is what, in grateful response to Marcus, Dom, and Steve, I now seek to do.

## The Five Pillars

In my opening contribution I gave five reasons for adopting the hypothesis that Jesus was a millenarian prophet who thought God's salvific transformation of the world to be near. I urged that this hypothesis, although generated prior to and apart from detailed analysis of the Jesus tradition, is then supported by such. Marcus, however, finds my pillars to be flawed, and Dom and Steve would no doubt agree. According to Marcus, I establish only the possibility of a Schweitzerian paradigm, not its probability. He is generous enough to say that both his Jesus and mine are, on initial inspection, equally plausible. It's just that mine fails to make the most sense of the sayings attributed to Jesus. But I'm unrepentant about my five points having more force than this.

1. The first point is that Jesus stands between the Baptist, with his announcement of eschatological judgment, and believers such as Paul, who thought the *parousia* to be near. Marcus counters by observing that Jesus differed from John in some respects, so why not here too? Well, of course this is possible, but probability remains on my side. There's an old and well-attested tradition that puts Jesus and John in parallel. One need only remember Luke 7:31–35 (for Q) and notice – here I give only a sampling – the parallelism between Mark 6:17–29 and Mark 14–15 (both John and Jesus are arrested, bound, executed, and laid in a tomb), between Luke 1:5–25, 57–80 and Luke 1:26–38; 2:1–52 (the infancy narratives for John and Jesus mirror each other), and Matt 3:2 and 4:17 (John and Jesus proclaim the very same message). This is a striking tradition in view of the Christian tendency to exalt Jesus over John, and surely the tradition originated because Jesus so much reminded people of John, whose central message seems to have been repentance in the face of eschatological judgment. Furthermore, Q 7:31–35 suggests that somebody took Jesus and John to have similar goals and proclamations, and that their differences were more in their delivery than in their substance. One infers the same from the certainty that Jesus underwent John's baptism: the act constitutes theological endorsement.

The endorsement is in fact so strong that Marcus, like Dom, Ernst Käsemann, and Maurice Goguel before him, imagines that Jesus originally accepted and even defended "John's vision of awaiting the apocalyptic God, the Coming One." Only later did he find it inadequate.[1] This is a surprising strategy to adopt,

---

1. Crossan, *The Historical Jesus*, 237–38.

because tracing developments in Jesus' thinking is usually reck-oned to be a discredited, old-fashioned thing. Besides, if Jesus was at one time a defender of apocalyptic, why does Marcus attrib-ute all the apocalyptic items in the tradition to the early church? Why not assign some of them to his stage 1 Jesus? His view con-cedes that my Jesus was in fact the historical Jesus, just not the mature Jesus. Further, by rejecting my interpretation of so much, Marcus seems to presuppose that the Jesus tradition represents almost exclusively his stage 2 Jesus. Why? Couldn't Marcus accept much of my reconstruction without jeopardizing his own? I don't myself think this is the way to go (because I don't buy the evi-dence for his stage 2), but I'm not sure why he doesn't consider this possibility, or why someone else couldn't surmise that Jesus' John the Baptist phase came later, not earlier.

Marcus envisages Jesus departing from John's apocalypticism and then some believers in Jesus later picking up that apocalypti-cism. But this posits two discontinuities: Jesus rejected John's apocalypticism, then some of Jesus' followers rejected that rejec-tion. My reconstruction more simply posits a continuity that is in line not only with John's baptism of Jesus but with the fact that Christianity's oldest extant document explicitly attributes its apoc-alyptic scenario to Jesus himself (1 Thes 4:13–5:11, see 4:15). Isn't my view also supported by the sayings that have Jesus praise John (e.g., Q 7:28 – no one born of women is greater than John the Baptist)?

2. Marcus upholds his postulate of dual discontinuity by sug-gesting – again I am reminded of Käsemann – that belief in Jesus' resurrection and post-Easter experience of the Spirit brought back to the Jesus movement the sort of eschatology earlier characteris-tic of the Baptist. But doesn't this beg the question? Why did believers choose language with so many eschatological associa-tions? The words "spirit" and "resurrection" weren't given with the experiences themselves but must be reckoned interpretations of those experiences.

My belief, following Schweitzer, is that eschatological language suggested itself because Jesus' followers went to Jerusalem with fervent eschatological expectations already in place; and this is the force of my second and third points. Marcus argues instead that Jews who experienced Jesus after his death as a living reality and continuing presence would not have talked about ghosts or resuscitation but resurrection. But half of the Jewish texts from 200 B.C.E.–100 C.E. that speak of an afterlife do it without mentioning the resurrection, and there was no single idea about life after death in that period but instead great variety. Immortality of the soul or something akin to it is found as often as not, and resurrection is not widely attested in texts before the time of Jesus. It would have been easy enough for Jesus' followers to declare that God had vindicated him without using the concept of the eschatological resurrection. They could have said, to borrow from Jubilees 23:31, that while his bones rested for now in the earth, his spirit was exalted in heaven.[2] Or they could have spoken about Jesus the way the Testament of Job, without using the language of resurrection, speaks about its hero: Job was enthroned in heaven immediately after his death.[3] Believers in Jesus might also, like some later so-called heretics, have concluded that their leader had only seemed to die, and that in reality he had ascended to heaven in the manner of Enoch and Elijah. For all I know, maybe all of these interpretations and still others were indeed offered soon after the crucifixion. But that would not undo the fact that many influential followers of Jesus, when proclaiming his vindication, instead used *anastasis nekrōn* (see Acts 4:2; Rom 1:4; 1 Pet 1:3), a technical term for the eschatological "resurrection of the dead."[4]

Why did they do this? Why did they use a technical term whose traditional contents matched so poorly the case of Jesus? The resurrection of the dead, when it appears in Jewish sources, is a collective experience, not something that happens to an isolated individual (which is why some early Christians tried their best not to isolate Jesus' experience: Matt 27:51–53; 1 Cor 15:20; Col 1:18). Resurrection is also associated with a number of supernatural events, such as the last judgment, which clearly had not yet occurred. To repeat, then, whereas Marcus thinks resurrection language was natural, I think it was peculiar.

My view is supported by what I have been able to learn about Sabbatai Sevi, a seventeenth-century Jewish messiah. His followers, who believed in the disappearance of their messiah's body and soul, said that his death wasn't a real death, that it was a mystery, that he would soon return, that he was exalted and hidden, that he had ascended to the supernal lights, and that he had gone

2. See Testament of Abraham A 20:10–11; Pseudo-Philo 32:9; Apocalypse of Moses 37–38. This was also said about Muhammad immediately after his death.

3. See 2 Macc 7:36, where eternal life is gained immediately after death, despite the resurrection being future: 12:43–44.

4. See 4Q521; Matt 22:31; 1 Cor 15:12; Did 16:6; and the rabbinic *těḥîyyat hammētîm*.

to the distant land of the lost ten tribes. Nowhere do we read that they ever said that God had raised Sabbatai from the dead. The same generalization may also hold for some other Jewish messiahs, including Abū Isa (eighth century), Shlomo Molkho (sixteenth century), and Shukr Kuhayl I (nineteenth century). I am familiar with stories of each of these escaping or in some way transcending death, but nowhere do I recall reading that anyone ever proclaimed their (past as opposed to future) resurrection. I find the same thing in Islamic stories about this or that Mahdi (e.g., Abū Hāshim and Mūsā al-Kāzim): the tale is, as far as my knowledge goes, always about disappearance; resurrection belongs to the future.

Further, if apparitions and other ostensible encounters with the dead are, as they seem to be, common place and cross-cultural, and if such encounters were, as Marcus claims, so naturally understood by Jews as "resurrection," one wonders why Jewish tradition isn't teeming with accounts of "resurrection."

3. When Marcus says that, "from the post-Easter vantage point, Jesus' death and resurrection marked the turning of the ages, so it is not surprising that they used eschatological language to express this conviction,"[5] I again want to ask, But why did they use precisely this language? Why on earth did people think that the ages had turned? This application of eschatological language about the end of world to the end of Jesus reminds me of what one so often finds in millenarian movements, which tend to read history in the light of their own eschatological expectations. When Jesus failed to come at the time calculated by William Miller, a nineteenth-century American preacher, some of the faithful said that their Lord had indeed come – but instead of arriving on earth, he entered the heavenly sanctuary and inaugurated a new phase of salvation history. The Seventh Day Adventists have dealt with their failed prophecies similarly. More recently, members of a Baha'i sect known as Baha'is Under the Provisions of the Covenant circulated a prophecy predicting for 1991 massive earthquakes and a meteor striking the earth. When nothing came to pass, their leader explained that there had been a "spiritual earthquake" created by the apostasy of an important member, and that "everything happens on the spiritual plane before it manifests in the physical plane." Rude reality reinterprets prophecies. I suggest

5. Above, p. 38.

similarly that Jesus' disciples went up to Jerusalem with eschatological expectations and thus they interpreted his crucifixion and
his post-mortem appearances as eschatological events. They corre-
lated Jesus' suffering and victory over death with the fundamental
pattern of Jewish eschatology, which is tribulation followed by
victory.

4. What then of my fourth point, that expectations like those
of the Baptist were widespread in Jesus' Jewish world? Here
Marcus rightly says that the prevalence of a particular belief is no
sure indication that Jesus held it. But is it fallacious to think that
the more prevalent a belief appears to have been in Judaism, the
more likely it is that Jesus might have shared it? That is all I was
trying to show. Wouldn't the plausibility of my case be dimin-
ished if I were to attribute to Jesus something that wasn't in the
air? Further, isn't it a reasonable hypothesis that Jesus heard and
believed Daniel as well as the many prophecies in the Hebrew
Bible that foretell the influx of the Diaspora, the transformation
of the land of Israel into a paradise, and Israel's spiritual renewal?
Even Philo was not altogether free of such hopes and dreams.[6]
Surely it is significant that many of the beliefs characteristic of
apocalyptic eschatology – the messianic woes, the universal judgment, the resurrection of the dead, punishment in Gehenna, cosmic renewal – regularly appear not only in many early Christian
texts but also in rabbinic sources. These shared beliefs obviously
have a common origin, which can't be anything other than first-
century Judaism, where they must have been regular religious
coin.

5. Finally, what of my fifth point, which is that our sources say
that outsiders compared Jesus to Theudas, to Judas the Galilean,
and to John the Baptist, people who had intense eschatological
expectations? Unlike Marcus, I don't consider this a variant of my
first point, which is about a line of continuity from John to Paul
through Jesus, not the explicit comparisons of Jesus to others: if
Jesus was not like those three people, who hoped for the imminent and supernatural redemption of God's people, then what
accounts for the comparisons?

Obviously I feel confident that my five points give good cause
for anticipating that the sayings tradition will show us a millenarian prophet. One of my earlier claims, however, I now qualify. In

---

6. See *Rewards and Punishments* 85–88, 177, 165–72.

my book I went so far as to say that, were the sayings to suggest some other result, the correct inference might be that the sayings tradition is unreliable, that Christians expunged from it the eschatological elements in order to protect Jesus from being viewed as a false prophet. One friendly reader of my manuscript recommended that I delete this judgment, and Steve Patterson has complained about it too.[7] I now recognize their wisdom and abandon my hyperbole. My five observations don't settle the matter of Jesus and eschatology. They rather generate a hypothesis that must be tested and filled out by a detailed analysis of the Jesus tradition. So the next question is, What do we make of that tradition?

## Trite Sayings and Contradictory Ideas?

Marcus says that my view of Jesus as a millenarian prophet makes the sayings tradition fall flat. He asks, for example, what Jesus meant, according to the apocalyptic paradigm, by teaching that true piety is inward, not outward. "Does this mean we will be judged at the last judgment on the basis of 'inner purity,' not outward observance?" And does the example of the good Samaritan teach that it is "important to be a neighbor and act compassionately because the judgment is at hand?" Again, within my paradigm, did Jesus' inclusive meal practice "mean simply, 'When the judgment and the messianic banquet have arrived, these folks will be included, so I'm including them now?'"

These questions are helpful, because they allow me to clarify my position. Marcus dismisses readings that I don't recognize as my own. An apocalyptic framework is a framework, not the whole picture. I have never thought that everything in the original Jesus tradition was generated by belief in a near end. Apocalyptic thinkers need not be monomaniacs. Although Martin Luther performed all his deeds in the conviction that the end was near, it would be silly to think that one could reduce all of the teachings of the great reformer in the way Marcus suggests my view reduces Jesus. And if we don't countenance such reductionist readings for Luther or Muhammad or (despite Matthew's apocalyptic content) the Sermon on the Mount, if we don't reduce to one idea everything written by James Usher, Jeremiah Burroughs, Billy Graham or the hundreds of others who have thought the end to be near,

7. Review of Allison's *Jesus*.

then why should anyone do this with Jesus? Why must apocalyptic be the enemy of polyvalence and imagination?

Consider, as a parallel, the interpretation of Matthew and Mark. These two Gospels are full of apocalyptic expectations, and their authors probably thought that the end was near. Despite this, no commentator ancient or modern known to me has given their lines the sorts of reductionistic readings that Marcus does. Certainly they aren't found in my own commentary on Matthew. Where did Marcus get them?

My sense is that while some of Jesus' instructions to those who followed him were motivated by his near expectation – here I think of some of the instructions to missionaries and some of the teachings on money – and while his eschatological expectations certainly added urgency to his demands, he drew most of his teaching from the well of Jewish tradition. That is, he taught and revised the law, the prophets, and the writings and the traditions that grew up around them. When Marcus says that Jesus' "animating vision flowed out of his experience of the sacred, his familiarity with the traditions of Israel . . . and his observation of the conditions of peasant life,"[8] I agree and don't understand why this is a point against me. I recall that 4 Baruch and the Testaments of the Twelve Patriarchs, which long for the end, are filled with conventional Jewish wisdom and exhortations to do Torah. Millenarian movements may be radical, but they are typically nativistic and so often emphasize the value of an indigenous cultural heritage or selected portions of it. Jesus is not an exception.

Marcus might want to protest that this makes no sense, that belief in a near end should cast out everything not directly related to eschatology. But while that might stand to reason, it just does not stand up to the facts. Anyone can walk into a so-called Christian bookstore and find shelves of books announcing that the end is near. The very same bookstore will also feature books concerned with long-term issues, such as what the future holds for our children. Not only are such books found in one place and often read by the same people, but some of each come from the same publishers and even the same authors. This appears irrational to those of us in the academy, but the real world does not submit to reason. Menachem Schneerson, the Lubavitcher Rebbe who died in 1994, was announcing the imminence of the

8. Above, p. 48.

Messiah's coming while simultaneously denouncing Palestinian autonomy because it would eventually lead to a Palestinian state.

Consistency is the hobgoblin of non-apocalyptic minds. Millenarian prophet after millenarian prophet illustrates Emerson's remark that "with consistency a great soul has simply nothing to do" as well as his advice to "speak what you think today in words as hard as cannon-balls, and to-morrow speak what to-morrow thinks in hard words again, even though it contradicts every thing you said to-day." The failure of prophets to be consistent should make one wary of a hermeneutic intolerant of tension. Thus, unlike Marcus, I don't think that if Jesus was a social prophet that he couldn't have been an apocalyptic prophet. Weren't Muhammad and Menachem Schneerson both? Didn't Akiba concern himself with both halakah and messianism? Nor do I see any reason to doubt that my eschatological Jesus was, to recall Marcus' multi-stroke sketch, a "Spirit person," a healer and exorcist, an enlightened wisdom teacher with unconventional wisdom, and a movement initiator. I long ago learned from my teacher, W. D. Davies, that "the 'Jesus' of Harnack and the 'Christ' of Schweitzer need not be mutually irreconcilable, but can be one and the same Person."[9]

The tension between near expectation and a long-term mentality focused on convention and on-going life characterizes millenarian movements from many times and places, so it needs no special explanation when it shows up also in the Jesus tradition. The rule is that millenarian prophets are consistently inconsistent. They just don't, for example, seem to feel any tension between what we call wisdom and apocalyptic. So why should such an antithesis play a role in my reconstruction of Jesus? Rejecting the apocalyptic side of Jesus because the other side uttered wisdom sayings and gave moral instruction for everyday life is no more persuasive than Walter Schmithals's contrary argument that the wisdom sayings can't go back to Jesus because he was in fact an apocalyptic prophet.

I wonder to what extent some who reject my sort of Jesus aren't operating with an understanding of apocalyptic that generates several additional antitheses that I question. When, for example, Steve says, in contrasting the parables of Jesus with apocalyptic (and so with my Jesus) that "the open, multivalent quality of Jesus'

9. Davies, "Apocalyptic and Pharisaism," 30.

parables stands in stark contrast to the typically closed, fixed quality of apocalyptic," I'm uneasy. It's not just that Steve is contrasting Jesus' parables with some idea of apocalyptic in general rather than with what I have said about Jesus' eschatology in particular. The main problem is that Steve is offering a generalization made earlier by Norman Perrin[10] — and didn't John Collins rightly question it?[11] Even in Daniel, where we get interpretive equations — the four great beasts of Daniel 7 are, for example, the kingdoms of Babylon, Medea, Persia, and Greece — the equations don't adequately express the seer's intent, for they don't have the allusive and evocative power of the vision. Daniel 7 also leaves much unexplained, such as the "great sea" of vv. 2–3. Indeed, apocalypses are full of mysteries and indeterminacy (witness the conflicting interpretations of John's Apocalypse), and they can even reveal that some things can't be revealed (e.g. Mark 13:32 and parts of 4 Ezra). Further, Daniel and its relatives are loaded with mythology and symbols of transcendent realities, things I don't think of as "closed" or "fixed." Daniel's bizarre beasts may have a one-to-one relationship to particular things — this beast is that kingdom — but the monsters, clouds, and others images communicate much more than this. So for me Steve's contrast between the open and the closed is not clearly a contrast between Jesus' parables and apocalyptic literature, much less apocalyptic eschatology.

Again, when Steve says that "the whole point of apocalyptic literature is to reveal to initiates the secret of how exactly the end will unfold," I want to say, No, that's not quite right. Certainly if that's apocalyptic, then we shouldn't associate Jesus with it. But when I think of 4 Ezra, 2 Baruch, and the Apocalypse of Abraham, I don't find these books to have one point or one meaning. They do a lot more than unfold the secrets of the end. So while I understand the contrast that Steve draws, I don't think it's clearly illustrated by Jesus and apocalyptic.

This leads to the important question of definition. I wrote one draft of *Jesus of Nazareth: Millenarian Prophet* without once using the word, "apocalyptic." An expert in second temple Judaism, however, encouraged me to use it, and my respect for him persuaded me. Unfortunately, its inclusion has hindered understand-

10. See "Wisdom and Apocalyptic."
11. See "The Symbolism of Transcendence."

ing. So many scholars have made so many generalizations about apocalyptic and apocalyptic literature (many of them negative), and so many of these generalizations have so little to do with the original Jesus tradition, that my position may strike many as unlikely before they even get to my arguments.

But I defined "apocalyptic" neither as that which characterizes the written apocalypses nor as a movement in ancient Judaism but as "apocalyptic eschatology," a cluster of eschatological themes and expectations – cosmic catastrophe, resurrection of the dead, universal judgment, heavenly redeemer figures, etc. – that developed, often in association with belief in a near end, in post-exilic Judaism. And I made it clear that, in my view, if Jesus taught about eschatological tribulation, the final judgment, the resurrection of the dead, and the restoration of Israel, and if in addition he reckoned those things to be near, then that's enough for me to call him an apocalyptic prophet. Obviously, however, if one thinks that "apocalyptic" must include esoterism, numerology, mythological beasts, and all sorts of other things found in the literary apocalypses but not in the original Jesus tradition, then there can be no argument: "apocalyptic" is the wrong word for Jesus.

Let me also add that to define is to classify, and that classifying an historical phenomenon on the basis of shared characteristics rather than peculiarities can distort. So to label Jesus a millenarian prophet who shared an "apocalyptic eschatology," as I have done, has its risks. It focuses attention on a sociological construct and what Jesus shares with others. But my purpose in all this is purely heuristic, not reductionistic. I've never thought that by making Jesus out to be a millenarian prophet I've said everything important or interesting about him.

## The Idea of Progress

Steve's chapter implies that I'm not quite up to speed, that the discipline is leaving me behind. I have not accepted "the most recent results of historical-critical research." Recent trends "have had little impact" on me. Indeed, I "mistrust . . . historical critical work as the basis for historical Jesus research." Further, in what appears to be an intended contrast with myself, Steve testifies that "historical critical arguments have meant something" to him. He has slogged "through the muck of historical critical scholarship alongside colleagues who forced me to take their arguments seriously." And "the distinctive voice of Jesus has begun to emerge from the careful critical analysis of the sources, from exegesis, from the problems and solutions suggested by the details of the texts themselves."[12]

I don't deny Steve's autobiography, but if he is implying that those who differ from him, including myself, do so because they have not heeded contemporary historical-critical research, or have not engaged in a careful critical analysis of the sources, or have not slogged through the muck of historical critical scholarship alongside their colleagues, or have not done exegesis or paid attention to the details of texts, then I don't know what to say. I leave it to others to judge whether such a generalization fairly characterizes my own biography. But if all Steve is saying is that he developed his big picture of Jesus after looking at the details of the tradition, then I'd like to ask him, Did you really manage to look at the details without having any hypothesis about the big picture? My impression is that there is always a dialectic between the details and the big picture; and when writing the first chapter of my Jesus book, I was just suggesting that we have some good reasons for starting with the big picture of Jesus as a millenarian prophet. I nowhere said that we must end there, and have never done so in my own work. Rather, as suggested above, the big picture is my initial hypothesis, which is like a frame without the picture. It has to be filled in by the details (which my Jesus book just begins to do, so maybe at points it necessarily distorts through omission).

Steve equates the works that support the direction of his research with the progress of our discipline, and one can certainly interpret the course of scholarship as leading to Steve's Jesus. There was first Ernst Käsemann, then Hans Conzelmann, then Philipp Vielhauer, then recognition of the importance of the Gospel of Thomas, then the North American discussion of the parables, then John Kloppenborg's stratification of Q, and then the Jesus Seminar. But it would be just as easy to construe a competing line of progress that starts with Schweitzer and includes Joachim Jeremias and E. P. Sanders, wouldn't it? Advance is in the eyes of the beholder, and Steve and I are different beholders. Let me offer three examples.

---

12. Above, p. 82.

1. Steve writes that "Vielhauer's tradition-historical work showed that all of these sayings [the synoptic Son of man sayings] (save one, Matt 24:37–39: here the matter remains undecided) are products of later Christian tradition."[13] I would have said that Vielhauer tried to show this regarding the (future) Son of man sayings, not that he did in fact show it. Certainly if one may judge by the flood of books and articles written since Vielhauer's contribution, most doubt that he settled the matter. A recent review of the critical literature on the Son of man makes it clear that all sorts of opinions were held in the past and that all sorts of opinions are held in the present.[14] Why, if Vielhauer was so persuasive, do so many who don't trace any apocalyptic Son of man sayings to Jesus not just reproduce his demonstration? Dom, in his big book on Jesus, doesn't do this but rather develops his own argument.

2. Steve says that "Kloppenborg's work demonstrated that, at least in the development of the Q tradition," there was a "pre-apocalyptic stage."[15] I would have said that Kloppenborg sought to demonstrate this, not that he did. How could I say anything else, given that I'm the author of a rival compositional history of Q, a history that doesn't posit such a "pre-apocalyptic stage"?[16] The problem is not that I have ignored Q research, or even that I haven't speculated about the stages of Q (I have − more than many of my colleagues think is warranted). It's just that Kloppenborg hasn't persuaded me that the units he designates as sapiential represent the initial or even a distinct stage of Q's development. There are, of course, prominent Q scholars who also remain unpersuaded that Kloppenborg must be followed in his delineation of $Q^1$, $Q^2$, and $Q^3$. Christopher Tuckett, Richard Horsley, and Alan Kirk (Kloppenborg's own student) come to mind.

Steve says that "Dale is generally skeptical . . . of Q research." Since I have defended the existence of Q at length in a three-volume commentary on Matthew, since I have written an entire book on Q that interacts with the work of others and features a reconstruction of its compositional history, and since I have written yet

---

13. Above, pp. 70–71.
14. Burkett, *The Son of Man Debate*.
15. Above, p. 73.
16. Allison, *The Jesus Tradition in Q*.

a second book on Q's scriptural intertextuality,[17] I can only conclude that Steve equates "Q research" with the conclusions of
Kloppenborg. With all due respect, isn't this a bit parochial?

3. Steve says that Dom and Burton Mack "have shown that the
reign of God is not an apocalyptic concept in ancient Judaism." I
would have written that they have observed that "kingdom (of
God)" could also be a sapiential expression, as it is in the Wisdom
of Solomon, Philo, and the Sentences of Sextus. But what should
we make of the following Jewish references to the kingdom of
God?

- Daniel 7:14: "To him [the one like a son of man] was
  given . . . the kingdom . . . . his kingdom will never be
  destroyed."
- Psalm of Solomon 17:3: "The kingdom of our God [*hē
  basileia tou theou* – the exact expression so often used in the
  New Testament] is forever over the nations in judgment."
- Testament of Moses 10:1: "And then his [God's] kingdom
  shall appear throughout his creation, and then Satan shall
  be no more, and sorrow shall depart with him."
- Sibylline Oracles 3:46–48, 767: "But, when Rome shall rule
  over Egypt . . . then the mightiest kingdom of the immortal
  king over men shall appear. . . And then indeed he will raise
  up his kingdom for all ages."
- 4Q246: "His kingdom will be an everlasting kingdom and
  all his ways in truth. He will judge the earth in truth and all
  will make peace. The sword will cease from the earth and all
  provinces will worship him. . ."
- 4Q521: "He will glorify the pious on the throne of an eternal kingdom."
- 1QSb IV.25–26: "May you attend upon the service in the
  Temple of the kingdom and decree destiny in company with
  the Angels of the Presence."
- The Kaddish prayer: "May he establish "his kingdom in your
  lifetime and in your days, and in the lifetime of the whole
  house of Israel, speedily and at a near time."
- The targums to the prophets, where "the kingdom of the
  Lord will be revealed" is characteristic.

17. Allison, *The Intertextual Jesus.*

Dom himself cites two of these texts and says that "'kingdom of God' could have been easily heard as an apocalyptic expression at the time of Jesus."[18] Moreover, isn't it a point in my favor that, unlike the texts I have just quoted, none of the sapiential kingdom texts is Palestinian?

Steve and I could of course debate a host of other issues. He says that, once he found his Jesus, the Gospel of John, with its realized eschatology, "now no longer seemed to appear from out of nowhere." But John 21:23 ("The rumor spread in the community that this disciple would not die. Yet Jesus did not say to him that he would not die, but, 'If it is my will that he remain until I come, what is that to you?'") offers a transparent reinterpretation of an unfulfilled eschatological prophecy (see Mark 9:1); and, whatever the relationship between John 21 and the rest of the Gospel, this is what I see throughout John. In John 2:13–25, for example, the Jerusalem temple becomes Jesus' body, and in 16:21, "the messianic woes and the joy attending the final salvation of the people of God . . . [are] understood in terms of the passion and resurrection of Christ."[19] John is the spiritualization of eschatology, a phenomenon which regularly appears in millenarian movements that survive disappointed expectations. The apocalyptic expectations of the nineteenth-century self-proclaimed Sudanese Mahdi, Muhammad Ahmad, were, against all the facts, turned into "realized eschatology:" "He filled the earth with equity and justice. . . . He destroyed oppression and those who caused it, and extirpated falsehood root and branch. The land was good and the people had rest. Islam cast its burdens to the earth, and justice spread far and wide."

Again, Steve more than once contrasts the presence of the kingdom with its futurity, and in private correspondence he has stressed that Luke 17:20–21 and Thomas 3 and 113 are keys to his reconstruction of Jesus. But millenarian movements are often marked by a fractured logic when it comes to the tension between fulfillment and expectation. Menachem Schneerson said that the king Messiah "will come" and, in the very same sentence, said he "is already here," and the Zionist R. Abraham Kook – who replaced the famous statement in *b. Sanh.* 98a that the Son of David will come in a generation that is entirely innocent or

18. Crossan, *The Historical Jesus*, 287.
19. Dodd, *Historical Tradition*, 373.

entirely guilty with the irrational proposition that the present generation is entirely guilty and entirely innocent – identified the
present with both the blessed time of the redemption and the
period of the messianic woes. So I'm unsure how consistent Jesus
must have been. But quite aside from this, the issue for me is
whether Jesus could have said something that accounts for Luke
17:20–21 and Thomas 3 and 113 and whether that something
plainly contradicts his belief in the presence of eschatological
tribulation and his hope in the nearness of the final judgment,
the resurrection of the dead, and the restoration of Israel. Is Steve
contrasting what lies behind Luke 17:20–21 and Thomas 3 and
113 not with my Jesus in particular but with stereotypes about
apocalyptic literature, including maybe Mark 13 (which I don't
think and didn't argue gives us an accurate picture of Jesus' eschatology)?

But enough. It's clear that there are several hypotheses which,
if Steve is right about them, should cause me to change my mind.
Steve must be puzzled and frustrated that I don't buy into them.
He must think me rather old-fashioned, or perhaps even an obscu-
rantist. From my point of view, his propositions remain too frag-
ile to build upon. One of us, it appears, is like the one-time
enthusiastic supporters of N-rays and steady state cosmology, aca-
demics who pursued promising but ultimately abandoned
hypotheses.

One final point about Steve's response. He makes much of his
having developed his views in "an open forum of scholars," which
prevents one from getting away with "uncritical assumptions.
Subjective judgments also become a pretty hard sell under that
sort of critical scrutiny."[20] He has in mind the Jesus Seminar. Now
although I clearly don't endorse their voting record, I don't deride
the Seminar. I'm sure Steve's experience in the group has been
quite educational, and there are certainly dangers in being the biblical studies equivalent of what Martin Gardner once called the
"hermit scientist." I do, however, ask whether there is another side
to sitting at table with others. Steve confesses that "it is hard to
dismiss Kloppenborg's work on Q when he is sitting there next to
you presenting an exceedingly plausible explanation for what you
are seeing in the text. It is difficult to overlook the significance of
the parables when Bernard Brandon Scott (*Hear, Then, the Parable*)

20. Above, p. 81.

is across the table from you forcing the issue."[21] Exactly so. What would have happened if Scott and Kloppenborg had never joined the Seminar, and if E. P. Sanders and Christopher Tuckett had joined instead? Maybe, if Steve had sat next to the latter two for a decade, his views would be the same, but one wonders. It's human nature to give more attention and respect to those we talk to and eat with than to the faceless people who mutely speak in books. Is Steve then trusting that the Seminar just happened to attract those with the best opinions?

## More Antitheses

I end this chapter by commenting on four of Dom's six antitheses: destructive or transformative, material or social, primary or secondary, negative or positive. (I will touch on the last two of Dom's anitheses – passive or active, instantive or durative – in Chapter 5.)

### Destructive or transformative?

Here I think we agree. Millenarian visions are typically theodicies, mythological ways of wrestling with evil within a religious worldview, and they console and inspire by imagining a world transformed by good triumphant. Now of course the arrival of such a world must mean the defeat of everything opposed to it, so millenarian visions regularly envisage the destruction of all that doesn't conform to the divine will. One cannot have the one without the other. "Long live the king!" comes only after "The king is dead." The correlate of redemption is doomsday, a day of darkness, not light (Amos 5:18). And often, sadly, the expectation of doom turns into anger, vengeance, and violence, as in many peasant revolts. The literature can be horrible, as when the blood rises as high as the horse's bridle in Rev 14:20, or when Lactantius writes in the fourth century that the godless shall be annihilated, and torrents of blood will flow (*Divine Institutes* 7.20). In the Jesus tradition, however, there is no blood. This is because with Jesus the emphasis is upon restoration, not destruction, and the motive is hope, not vengeance. Luke 9:51–56, where James and John are rebuked for wanting to call fire down from heaven, catches the

21. Above, p. 81.

spirit of Jesus. His eschatology is not an expression of resentment but of hope in Israel's God.

## Material or social?

In responding to my emphasis upon the literal nature of many millenarian forecasts, Dom wants to know "what is necessary, unnegotiable, and essential; what is unnecessary, negotiable, and unessential." His conviction is that what mattered above all to the ancients was not falling stars or other celestial escapades but the arrival of lasting, universal justice, social utopia. I won't argue against this either because it's obviously right. One does, in parts of 1 Enoch, run into a real interest in cosmological states, but that is rare, and it is certainly foreign to Jesus. We may safely presume that eschatological earthquakes, although literally expected, would in themselves have meant little. The cosmological forecasts were ways of saying that things were so wrong that they couldn't be righted without radical change. They were an expression of a deep-seated pessimism about the world as it is, a world gone so bad that it needs a transcendent solution, and simultaneously an expression of a deep-seated confidence in God, who can fix the world by doing incredible things.

Two qualifications. First, our distinction between the essential and unessential is indeed ours; it is not spelled out in ancient texts. I'd guess that most ancients, like so many modern Christians, would not have thought to separate, let's say, the literalness of bodily resurrection from its theological meanings.

Second, I stressed the literal nature of apocalyptic forecasts because Tom Wright, who is now such a prominent Jesus researcher, stresses instead their metaphorical nature. Against this, I'm impressed by how literal millenarian movements tend to be, at least initially, about their prophecies, how seldom one runs into something like the Mu'tazila interpretation of Islamic eschatology, which turns everything into pure symbols. I'm also unconvinced that whoever first composed future Son of man sayings would have agreed with Tom that they were fulfilled in the destruction of Jerusalem in 70 c.e. The eschatological vision of the early Jesus tradition is a vision of utopia, and utopia has not come. So my case for literalism was an attempt to resist correlating Jesus' eschatological vision with anything history has had to offer. I was not trying to unfold the essence of apocalyptic eschatology, which for me is a transcendent and universal solution to the problem of evil.

To argue that a piece of language was understood literally is not to settle the question of meaning. For example, it's one thing to argue that Mark thought that the sun went dark when Jesus was crucified, quite another to decide whether that darkness was for him a symbol of mourning, a sign of judgment, an indication of the cosmic meaning of the crucifixion, a fulfillment of Amos 8:9, a portent typically associated with the death of heroes, or some combination of these.

### Primary or secondary?

Dom's third antithesis is between what he calls primary apocalypticism, which "demands immediate actions of extraordinary ethics because of the expectation of imminent consummation," and what he calls "secondary apocalypticism," which "demands immediate actions or extraordinary ethics because of the permanent character and abiding revelation of God. This is how one should be living and what one should be doing here and now in any case and apocalyptic imminence is sanction rather than cause."[22] As I have already indicated, while some of the imperatives in the Jesus tradition are in Dom's sense primary – again I think of instructions to missionaries and words about money – most of them are secondary. This is because the nearness of the end does not of itself generate moral imperatives. I know a man who claims that he would sin in new ways if he thought he had little time left, because he then wouldn't have to suffer the consequences. The imminence of the end is just like being hanged in a fortnight – it may be, as Samuel Johnson observed, an effective way of concentrating the mind, but it doesn't generate a moral tradition. So how one responds to the end depends on the tradition within which one already stands. In Judaism that tradition has always been Torah. So the Jewish apocalypses often function like the rabbinic exhortation to repent a day before one's death. Apocalypses may offer new revelations, but they also seek to get people to do what they already know they should be doing but aren't. 1 Enoch 99:2 says: "Woe to those who pervert the words of truth and transgress the everlasting law." The Torah is also the

---

22. Above, p. 61.

exalted norm in 2 Baruch (38:2, etc.), the Testament of Moses (12:10–11), and the Testaments of the Twelve Patriarchs (Testament of Levi 13:2, etc.). It's always possible, as happened especially in medieval Jewish messianic movements, for antinomianism to raise its ugly head. But that is not characteristic of the old Jewish apocalypses. Nor, despite the tension between Torah and some of his more provocative utterances (e.g., Q 9:60 [Leave the dead to bury their own dead] and 14:26 [Hate father and mother]), was Jesus in any real sense an antinomian.

The apocalyptic depiction of God's goal for creation is a way of depicting God's will, a will that belongs to the present as well as to the future, a will that has already been revealed in the Torah. The author of 2 Baruch would have agreed with Pascal that "All the good maxims are already current; what we need is to apply them." Millenarian prophets do, however, tend to be especially fond of those elements in their traditions that emphasize the transience of things. This is one reason why they, like Jesus, pick up ascetic elements and teachings about the fleeting nature of wealth. Despite this, if we accept Dom's definitions, in Judaism and the Jesus tradition "primary apocalypticism" is secondary while "secondary apocalypticism" is primary. I think of Paul. His remarks about marriage in 1 Corinthians 7 are partly governed by the nearness of the end, but most of the exhortations elsewhere in 1 Corinthians are not so governed. I also think of Amos Wilder, who thought of eschatology as a formal sanction of imperatives – an appeal to self-interest in view of the judgment – but not the essential sanction, which is appeal to the nature of God.[23]

By the way, this is why I'm not bothered in the least by Dom's observation that Christianity got stronger the longer it went wrong – a generalization that might be equally made about Seventh Day Adventism, Jehovah's Witnesses, or dozens of other millenarian movement that didn't die in infancy. Such movements carry within themselves much that speaks to people apart from the imminence of the end. I don't myself see any necessary link between Jesus' eschatology and, for instance, his confidence in God as father, his focus on intention, and much else.[24] And that

23. Wilder, *Eschatology and Ethics*, 133.
24. See Allison, *Jesus*, 46–49, where I directly associate with eschatology only seven or eight of seventeen themes prominent in the teaching of Jesus.

Christianity's success might be due less to its eschatological enthu-siasm and more to such other things is hardly an objection to my Jesus. Long before Jesus, Zoroastrianism was evidently born with the belief that the world was about to be consumed, and Zoroastrians remain with us to this day. Despite the extermina-tion of Thomas Münster's expectations at the battle of Frankenhausen in 1525, the *Hutterite Chronicle* praises his intelli-gence and doctrine; his influence remained. The Baha'is began as an Islamic Mahdist movement but soon enough became some-thing else. Paul too belongs here. For his theology, despite the unfulfilled expectations of 1 Thessalonians and his apocalyptic worldview, has spoken to many.

Millenarian movements again and again find various strategies to develop, to use the sociological jargon, a "culture of disso-nance-reduction," and one way of doing this is "goal displace-ment." Winston Churchill, without the jargon, quipped that people "occasionally stumble over the truth, but most of them pick themselves up and hurry off as if nothing had happened." So prophecies, even if formative, readily get ignored or reinterpreted. Nostradamus, who thought that the end was nigh four hundred and fifty years ago, is still in print and even gets his own TV spe-cials once in a while. In Sabbatianism, the date of the consumma-tion was originally 1666, but it was easily moved when required. The apocalyptic expectations of Muhammad Ahmad, who died in 1885, were just forgotten by his more modernist followers, who made him out to be a reformer of Islam and a Sudanese national-ist, "the father of independence." Don't people still hunt for clues to the future in an ancient book in which Jesus says, a full four times, "I come quickly" (Rev 3:11; 22:7, 12, 20)? It's not surpris-ing that there was never any debilitating crisis over the delay of the *parousia* in the early church (although I think that eschatolog-ical disillusionment fed Gnosticism), nor surprising that through the centuries many Christians have happily referred Matt 24:36–44 (watching for the Son of man) to death rather than to the *parousia* (so already Chrysostom in the fourth century). Millenarian movements are complex things, and they often have the resources to thrive despite failed forecasts. Further, the sociol-ogists now tell us that, to judge by interviews with those who have joined new religious movements, social factors usually matter far more than does ideology.

### Negative or positive apocalypse

Dom sets forth two different fates for Gentiles in the Jewish tradition – redemption and extermination. He then speaks of "the choice between human extermination or human conversion, between divine vengeance or divine justice and, ultimately, between transcendental violence or transcendental non-violence." How do I respond? Well, I'm not sure exactly what Jesus thought about us Gentiles. I'm firmly convinced that Q 13:28–29 (many will come from east and west) was originally about the return of exiles from the Jewish diaspora, and without that unit I see little evidence to go on, although (as Dom sees) the existence of an early mission to Gentiles strongly suggests that he didn't anticipate their eschatological annihilation.

It is my judgment, however, that Q 10:13–15 (the woes against Chorazin, Bethsaida, and Capernaum); Q 13:28 (those thrown out will weep and gnash their teeth); and Mark 9:43–48 (the sayings about the cutting off of limbs to avoid hell) are probably based on things Jesus said, so he evidently believed, with many Jews of his day, in some kind of hell. But given the undeveloped and various ideas of hell then current, we can't make many generalizations about what he must have thought about it.

What then do I have to say about hell? All I can say here is that finding the historical Jesus isn't the same thing as doing theology. I'm fond of Origen, Gregory of Nyssa, and Evagrius Ponticus, who were universalists. And I sympathize with the opponents of Augustine in *City of God* 21, who were uncomfortable with Augustine's sort of hell. I like Apocalypse of Peter 14 and Sibylline Oracles 2:330–339, where the righteous can pray people out of hell. I like the Greek Apocalypse of the Virgin and the Ethiopic Apocalypse of the Virgin, books in which hell is not in session on Sundays or between Easter and Pentecost respectively. And I especially like the Armenian version of the Apocalypse of Paul, where the prayers of Mary and Paul release all from torment. I share Dom's disbelief in transcendent vengeance, but I'd argue, not that Jesus himself didn't believe in judgment, but that he preached it out of concern for those he thought off track, and further that his characteristic teaching about nonviolence and love of enemy deconstructs the conventional hell of Christian tradition.

From another point of view, however, there is no denying hell – the temporal hells that multitudes have lived through on this earth when they have been tortured by violent people and abused by the brutal accidents of life. How do we line up this ugly reality with our faith that God must be gracious and good — not gracious and good in some general sense but good and gracious to every single individual human being who has ever lived? If this world is all that there is, then those who have been to hell and never come back are without reprieve, and this I can't believe. I don't agree with the English poet Alexander Pope that "whatever is, is right." I have to change Pope's tense: Whatever will be, will be right. That is, I believe that we must not only work for justice in this life but also, because our feeble work never comes close to accomplishing its goals, hope for justice in a world to come, in which all mourning and crying and pain are no more. Otherwise I have only Stoicism to share with my despairing friend whose pregnant wife has just been senselessly killed by a drunken driver. So I think Jesus had it right: he so thirsted for justice on such a grand scale that he had to embrace his tradition's belief in the transcendence of history and death. He may have been mistaken, but he wasn't wrong.

# Part 2:
# Taking Stock

## Chapter 4:
### Assessing the Arguments

Dale Allison
John Dominic Crossan
Marcus Borg
Stephen Patterson

# Assessing the Arguments

Dale Allison
Marcus Borg
John Dominic Crossan
Stephen Patterson

In this chapter the participants each answer four questions.

- What is the strongest point in my position?
- What is the weakest point in the other position?
- What is the strongest point in the other position?
- What is the weakest point in my position?
  OR I would feel more secure about my position if . . .

## DALE ALLISON

*What is the strongest point in my position?*

This is difficult, for I think of my argument as an example of what philosophers call abduction or inference to the best explanation. My hypothesis derives its force not from any single observation but from its ability to account for a variety of facts. Nonetheless, if I have to isolate one fact, I suppose it's my first pillar, which is that Jesus comes out of the Baptist movement and is immediately succeeded by followers with apocalyptic eschatology. The strength of the connection with the Baptist is such that at least Marcus and Dom concede that the apocalyptic Jesus was the historical Jesus, it's just that (they think) he later became something else.

I'm also impressed by the fact that the apocalyptic Jesus shows up in so many strands of the tradition – in Paul, in Q, in Mark, in M, in L, in John's tradition, and even in parts of the Gospel of Thomas (e.g., Thomas 111). Competing understandings of Jesus are indeed found in most of Thomas and John, and Steve also calls to witness Paul's opponents in 1 Corinthians and Kloppenborg's first stage of Q. But I have my doubts about Kloppenborg's compositional history of Q while the literature on 1 Corinthians leaves me rather confused about Paul's Corinthian opponents, and John strikes me as a clear example of the reinterpretation of an apocalyptic tradition. So I'm pretty much left with Thomas. I take it seriously as an early and often independent witness to the Jesus tradition, but I'm less impressed with its force because I don't see it as surrounded by a host of supporting witnesses. Perhaps, however, others could regard me as like the hopeless defenders of the Byzantine text, who appeal to superior numbers when the real question is one of antiquity.

*What is the weakest point in the other position?*

One large flaw in the case for the non-apocalyptic Jesus is the obvious: Jesus endorsed the apocalyptic Baptist and was followed by a religious movement that produced texts full of apocalyptic language and images. But as I've already made so much of this, I want briefly to reiterate another point, this being that the non-apocalyptic Jesus is regularly reconstructed from contrasts; that is, he often emerges as one half of what I deem to be a false dichotomy. Steve, for example, contrasts the presence of the kingdom with the future coming of the kingdom and makes Jesus a proponent of the former, not the latter; and Marcus contrasts the urgency of a social prophet with the urgency of an apocalyptic prophet and says that Jesus was one, not the other.

I find such dichotomies problematic as guides to finding the past. Not only do our sources for Jesus contain these and other seeming tensions — which means that at least Jesus' followers could abide them — but so do dozens of old Jewish writings as well as apocalyptic texts from almost all times and places. If the Lubavitcher Rebbe and his followers could speak of salvation as present and coming, and if in their writings there is no antithesis between apocalyptic urgency and social urgency, and if in such matters the Lubavitchers are not exceptional but rather typical, then eliminating the apocalyptic Jesus with a criterion of consistency doesn't make much sense. Simplistic contrasts that don't apply elsewhere cannot be a reliable means of sorting out who said what, or didn't say what. They cannot become evidence that Jesus was this or that *as opposed to* an apocalyptic prophet.

*What is the weakest point in my position?*

Let me mention two possible chinks in my eschatological armor. One is that there is an interesting parallel to the theory, which I reject, that Jesus began as an apocalyptic prophet but later grew out of it. The early sources for Muhammad, including the Qur'an, show the same sort of tension between imminent eschatological expectation and wisdom for the long term that we find in the Jesus tradition. Some have resolved this tension by positing that, although Muhammad began with a belief in the near end of the world, his focus changed as he got older. I think Marcus and Dom might wish to explore this analogy. I note, however, that there are historians of Islam who have no trouble thinking that the two different ways of looking at the world existed side by side in Muhammad at the same time, and that there is clear evidence that Ibn Ishāq and other influential historians of early Islam downplayed its apocalyptic character.

A more important weakness may be my failure to set forth what exactly I think about Luke 17:20–21 and Thomas 3 and 113. Steve has written to me that "I don't think we'd be having this debate if it weren't for Luke 17:20–21 and Thomas 3 and 113. If this tradition didn't exist, then my attention would not be drawn to the other evidence for a division in early Christianity over this issue of eschatology." Fair enough. So what's the response?

One option open to me is to deny that this tradition goes back to Jesus by affirming that Luke 17:20–21, which has no synoptic parallel, is Lukan redaction (the opinion of a few), and that Thomas' tradition depends upon Luke. But there are features in 17:21 that don't seem to be Lukan, so that's not the way to go. A better proposal would be to regard Luke 17:20–21 as closer to what Jesus said than either Thomas 3 or 113 and then follow a common exegesis of Luke 17:20–21, according to which *entos humōn* means not "within you" but "among you," and according to which the saying is, in agreement with the Pharisees' question, about the future ("And being asked by the Pharisees when the kingdom of God comes . . ."). Jesus is then saying that the kingdom, when it comes, comes suddenly and unexpectedly: "One moment the world is just its normal self: then Lo! the Kingdom of God is among you."[1] This would accord with the denial of signs

---

1. Manson, *The Sayings of Jesus*, 304.

in Luke (= Q) 11:29 and the stress on the sudden appearance of the end in Luke (= Q) 17:22–37, the discourse introduced by Luke (= Q) 17:20–21. It would also, as Johannes Weiss saw, make Jesus deny the sort of calculation of the end one finds in some apocalypses. But that is no more a problem for me than it was for Weiss. To hold that Jesus had an apocalyptic eschatology is not to say that he didn't disagree with some of the things we find in apocalypses.

There are, however, competing and equally plausible explanations of Luke 17:20–21 and its parallels in Thomas, and some of these explanations don't harmonize with an apocalyptic Jesus. So to satisfy Steve at least I need to offer a detailed analysis of this tradition and show, if possible, that the best tradition history of it coheres with my position. I have yet to do this.

*What is the strongest point in the other position?*

Here I'll be generous and say that my interlocutors have at least three things going for them. The first is the undoubted creativity of the Jesus tradition, a creativity manifest in the freedom with which Matthew and Luke rewrite Mark. Because there's no good reason to imagine that, in their handling of tradition, Matthew and Luke are anomalies, our task is not simple: we have to separate the redactional and apocryphal weeds from the original wheat. The fact that I can find my apocalyptic Jesus in several sources does not make him the historical Jesus. Christian tradition could, in theory, have invented him.

And it's not just that we see Matthew and Luke rewriting Mark. We also know, from personal experience as well as from critical studies, that a popular tradition, such as that about Jesus, is subject to exaggeration and distortion from the first. We have no reason to believe that the disciples of Jesus did not make their own contributions and alterations. One might even hazard (although I don't) that Jesus' disciples misunderstood some of what he said, as Mark wants us to believe. So the addition to the Jesus tradition of – or, from another point of view, its corruption by – apocalyptic elements is not at all hard to imagine.

The second point my thesis could do without is that early Christian literature (here incidentally like Islamic literature) shows us precisely such augmentation, a point Marcus stresses. The few sayings of Jesus that may lie behind Mark 13 have been overlaid with apocalyptic elements probably inspired by the crisis of the

40s and/or the crisis of the 60s. And Matthew's insertion of the apocalyptic refrain, "the weeping and gnashing of teeth" (Matt 13:42, 50; 22:13; 24:51; 25:30), is just one example of his enhancing the image of the apocalyptic Jesus. So the question is not whether apocalyptic elements were added at a secondary stage but the extent of the addition, and whether there were any such elements there in the first place.

My third point against myself is that, by throwing in with Schweitzer, I've not just set myself against the results of the Jesus Seminar and three of its prominent members. According to Marcus, "the apocalyptic Jesus dominated Jesus scholarship for much of the twentieth century."[2] Steve speaks similarly of "the century old consensus, made popular by Albert Schweitzer."[3] But don't these sorts of generalizations overestimate the dominance of the position I've taken? Can we really say, without fear of exaggeration, that Schweitzer was the Abraham of his day, that is, the father of a multitude? I don't think that Schweitzer ever brought about the sort of consensus that B. H. Streeter's book on the synoptic problem did. Otherwise we can't explain why the meaning of "kingdom of God" continued to be so hotly debated. C. H. Dodd, with his "realized eschatology," turned Schweitzer upside down while T. W. Manson scoffed at what he thought Schweitzer said about Jesus' "interim ethic," and Dodd and Manson were, for a very long time, the premiere English-speaking scholars of Jesus.

If we look to Germany, we find Ernst Käsemann saying, long before Dom and Marcus, that while Jesus came out of the Baptist movement, he eventually went his own non-apocalyptic way. And Käsemann was not alone. Klaus Koch could characterize much of twentieth-century continental New Testament scholarship as "the agonized attempt to save Jesus from apocalyptic."[4] A survey would show that William Sanday, E. von Dobschütz, B. W. Bacon, Maurice Goguel, C. J. Cadoux, John Wick Bowman, T. F. Glasson, Ernst Fuchs, Philipp Vielhauer, Hans Conzelmann, Ethelbert Stauffer, John A. T. Robinson, Eta Linnemann, George Caird, Norman Perrin, Bruce Chilton and a host of others have had serious reservations about Schweitzer's sort of Jesus or rejected it altogether. Richard Hiers, a defender of Schweitzer, was twenty years

2. Above, p. 31.
3. Above, p. 69.
4. Koch, *Rediscovery*, 67–97.

ago bemoaning the fact "that interpreters tend either to avoid or to interpret away any evidence suggesting that Jesus actually held or conducted himself in accordance with the eschatological ideas attributed to him in the synoptic gospels."[5] Before that, and speaking of things in Germany, August Strobel complained that "in the view of today's exegetes and New Testament scholars, the proclamation of Jesus and his followers was not actually intended apocalyptically. Its emphasis lay rather on the call to decision in the present, and the actual event of salvation occurred in Jesus' word."[6]

Marcus, Dom, and Steve are, in their doubts about the apocalyptic or millenarian Jesus, not upstarts but members of a long and distinguished line of interpreters. Schweitzer may have set the agenda, but he never came close to swaying everybody. My estimation is that the state of today's English-speaking academy is not that far from what it has been for a hundred years, that is, pretty much evenly divided for and against Schweitzer.

*I would feel more secure about my position if . . .*

That's easy. I'd feel a lot better if I didn't know about the three points I just made.

## MARCUS BORG

Because competing paradigms constitute the foundational difference between Dale and me, my perception of my strongest point and his weakest are closely related.

*What is the strongest point in my position?*

I cite two related features: comprehensiveness and explanatory power. *Comprehensiveness*: my sketch of Jesus as a Jewish mystic, healer and exorcist, enlightened wisdom teacher, social prophet, and movement founder enables me to accommodate a large amount of the material in the synoptic gospels. Moreover, the resulting sketch of Jesus is, I would say, "persuasively full" (which I know is not the same as "fully persuasive"). *Explanatory power*: its fullness has considerable explanatory power. It helps us to understand the remarkable impact Jesus had on his followers and

5. Hiers, *Jesus and the Future*, x.
6. Strobel, *Kerygma und Apokalyptik*, 12.

on the traditions that developed around him. I would argue that any sketch of Jesus that does not find him to be remarkable has got it wrong.

*What is the weakest point in the other position?*

For this point, the distinction I made earlier between primary and secondary apocalyptic[7] is crucial. Depending upon which of these Dale affirms, the major weakness in his position is somewhat different. Moreover, the issue is not peculiar to Dale's position in particular, but must be dealt with by any scholar who argues that Jesus had an apocalyptic eschatology.

The first possibility: Dale is arguing that apocalyptic eschatology was *primary* for Jesus. His expectation of God's imminent apocalyptic intervention, transformation of the world, resurrection of the dead, and final judgment was central to his message and mission. Very simply – but I trust not misleadingly – Jesus' message becomes primarily, "God's going to make everything right, and soon."

If this is Dale's position, the resultant *gestalt* of Jesus seems inadequate to account for his effects on those who followed him and on the developing traditions about him in the New Testament. Jesus doesn't seem very remarkable: he becomes another mistaken proclaimer of "God's going to fix everything soon." Moreover, it isn't a very full sketch. As I see things, Jesus combines features of an enlightened wisdom teacher like the Buddha with the God-intoxicated passion of a social prophet like Amos or Micah or Jeremiah. He seems to me to have much more in common with them than with millenarian figures like a cargo cultist or a Wovoka.

The second possibility: Dale is arguing that apocalyptic eschatology was *secondary* for Jesus. For secondary apocalyptic, the expectation of God's imminent intervention is one element in a fuller picture of Jesus. Not all of Jesus' teaching and activity needs to be seen as apocalyptically motivated. He was more than a millenarian prophet. But the more Dale allows other major emphases into Jesus' message and vision, the more his position moves toward secondary apocalyptic. And the more he does this, the less that "millenarian prophet" is functioning as a paradigm, and the

7. See above, p.44.

more misleading it becomes as a shorthand characterization of Jesus. It highlights that which is secondary

Of these two options, Dale's use of the language of "paradigm" suggests that he is arguing for primary apocalyptic. Paradigm means the primary lens, or primary gestalt, or primary framework within which to see the whole. I am not trying to pigeonhole him or back him into a corner. I would be happy to have him change his mind. But what I am saying is this: (1) if he is arguing for primary apocalyptic, much of the Jesus tradition remains unintegrated and/or unpersuasively interpreted; and (2) if he is arguing for secondary apocalyptic, then "millenarian prophet" is no longer a paradigm and not a good shorthand description of Jesus.

One final point: Dale's phrase "millenarian prophet" highlights that about which Jesus was most mistaken. Doing so, it seems to me, obscures much about Jesus. We see this in the epilogue to his book, where post-apocalypse justice becomes post-mortem justice. Because it so clearly illustrates the consequences of seeing Jesus through the lens of primary apocalyptic, I quote it at some length.

> Jesus is the millenarian prophet of consolation and hope who comforts those who mourn. He sees the poor, the hungry and the reviled, and he proclaims that the last will be first. He makes the best of a bad situation: things are not what they seem to be; everything will be OK. *He declares, against all the evidence, that the oppressed and the destitute are not miserable but blessed. They will have treasure in heaven. They will be rewarded at the resurrection of the just.*[8]

But, of course, the world continued quite unchanged:

> Jesus the millenarian prophet, like all millenarian prophets, was wrong: reality has taken no notice of his imagination. Was it not all a dream, an unfounded fantasy – a myth, in the derogatory sense of the word?[9]

And then, in his final paragraph, Dale writes:

> And yet, despite everything, for those who have ears to hear, Jesus the millenarian herald of judgment and salvation, *says the only things worth saying, for his dream is the only dream worth dreaming.* If our wounds

---

8. Allison, *Jesus*, 217, italics added.
9. Allison, *Jesus*, 218.

never heal, if the outrageous spectacle of a history filled with cataclysmic sadness is never undone, if there is nothing more for those
who were slaughtered in the death camps or for six year olds devoured
by cancer, then let us eat and drink, for tomorrow we die. *If in the end
there is no good God to calm this sea of troubles, to raise the dead, and to give
good news to the poor, then this is indeed a tale told by an idiot, signifying
nothing.*[10]

But are hopes for post-mortem justice and promises of a blessedness beyond death "the only things worth saying" and "the only
dream worth dreaming"? And if there is no post-mortem justice,
is life "indeed a tale told by an idiot, signifying nothing"?

I share Dale's horror about all of the premature and brutal
deaths that mark human history: babies and children and other
innocents dying from malnutrition, massacred in wars, sold into
slavery, brutalized beyond imagination. But I have two difficulties
with his epilogue. The first: I have difficulty imagining post-
mortem justice. I wish that I could. But I cannot imagine what it
means to say, "All the victims will live again in a state of blessedness" (presumably with the corollary that the perpetrators will not
share in the blessedness). The second concerns Jesus: I doubt that
Jesus' message about God and God's justice was primarily about
post-apocalypse or post-mortem justice. Yet this is the conclusion ·
to which the apocalyptic paradigm leads.

*What is the strongest point in the other position?*

The greatest strength in Dale's position is the reasonableness of
his primary assumption: that if John the Baptizer and early
Christianity both had an apocalyptic eschatology, so did Jesus. It
creates a plausible prima facie case.

Yet supposing an alternative plausible explanation is not as difficult as advocates of an apocalyptic paradigm suggest. I begin by
acknowledging that many first-century Christians did affirm an
apocalyptic Jesus: they believed that Jesus would return soon. Did
the author of Revelation think the second coming of Jesus was
near? Yes. Did the authors of Mark, Matthew, and Q think this
was near? Yes. Did Paul think so? Yes.

But I think there are good reasons to see early Christian apocalyptic eschatology as secondary instead of primary. I see it as secondary in both importance and origin. First, with the exception

10. Allison, *Jesus*, 219, italics added.

of Revelation, I see it as *secondary in importance*, not as the primary content of their proclamation. And even in the book of Revelation, the main theme seems to the lordship of Christ versus the lordship of Caesar.

Second, I see it as *secondary in origin*. It did not come from Jesus, but originated in the post-Easter community as the expectation of Jesus' return. Its origins, as I suggested earlier in this book, lie in the extraordinary impression that Jesus made on them during his lifetime, and in the Easter experience of Jesus as a living reality whom God had exalted to be Lord and Christ. Consequently, they believed that the apocalyptic consummation was at hand, and the form in which they expected it was the second coming of Jesus.

One more comment about continuity: though Dale's affirmation of apocalyptic continuity looks impressive, it actually creates problems of significant discontinuity between Jesus and the early Christian movement. As I shall argue in the next chapter, the characteristic emphases of early Christianity – its teaching about "the way," the shape of the community, its christology – become more difficult to explain if Jesus was primarily a millenarian prophet.

*I would feel more secure about my own position if . . .*

I didn't like it. I freely admit that I like the sketch of Jesus that I have drawn in several books. He strikes me as an utterly remarkable human being. I find his vision of life to be attractive, compelling, and challenging. Robert Funk, cofounder of the Jesus Seminar, has written, "Beware of a Jesus whom you like." There is insight in his remark: we often create gods and heroes by projecting our own deepest wishes onto them.

But sketching a Jesus who is remarkable and impressive and who tells me what is most important in life cannot in itself disqualify the sketch. Would we say of Buddhist scholars who find the Buddha and his teaching to be utterly remarkable, and who for that reason commit themselves to the way of the Buddha, that they are probably projecting their own ideals on to the Buddha? Or would we say, "There had to be something remarkable about the Buddha and his teaching, and understandings of the Buddha that suggest that there wasn't something remarkable are likely to be wrong."

Thus I cannot accept the notion that we can trust our "objectivity" as historians only if we find an unattractive Jesus, even as I recognize that the importance that Jesus has had in my life since earliest childhood disposes me to find a compelling Jesus.

## JOHN DOMINIC CROSSAN

Apart from the obvious conflict-of-interest and judge-in-one's-own-case problems of assessing strengths and weaknesses in our opposing positions, there is one other immediate problem. Your position, Dale, involves both the very clear and coherent thesis of your book but also the response you made here to my own arguments with it. Similarly for myself. My *permanent position* across thirty years of research and publication on the historical Jesus, from my 1973 *In Parables*[11] to my 1998 *The Birth of Christianity*[12] is: (1) that Jesus was eschatological but not apocalyptic, (2) that the former is a genus of which the latter is but one of its many species, and (3) that describing the precise content of such non-apocalyptic eschatology was a primary focus. I was, in other words, disagreeing with those who said he was neither eschatological nor apocalyptic, with those who said he was both eschatological and apocalyptic, as well as with those who thought that eschatology and apocalypticism were synonymous. I see my position of a non-apocalyptic eschatological Jesus as similar to that of Helmut Koester and John Kloppenborg Verbin. The best argument for that position, by the way, is not and never was the latter's proposed stratification of the Q Gospel ($Q^1$, $Q^2$, $Q^3$), which was explicitly asserted as a sequence of composition rather than tradition.[13] Instead, the best argument is Steve Patterson's stratification of that corpus of sayings common to and diversely redacted by the Q Gospel and the Gospel of Thomas.[14] *That* is an argument about sequence in tradition and not just in composition.

But my *present position* in this book did not repeat my *permanent* position. Instead, it attempted (1) to go inside your own position of an apocalyptic continuum from the Baptist, through Jesus, and on into Paul, the Q Gospel, and Mark, and insist (2) that you would have to make a series of distinctions within that alleged continuity in order to explain what actually happened in the first century. My reasons for adopting that method of debate are to

11. See pp. 25–27.
12. See pp. 257–87.
13. Kloppenborg, *The Formation of Q*, 244–45.
14. Patterson, "Wisdom."

make certain that (1) we do not argue without making the necessary distinctions and definitions, (2) we move the debate forward, and (3) we get to what is of ultimate importance for then and now. What, in other words, is the content and meaning of an apocalyptic Jesus, what is the content and meaning of a non-apocalyptic Jesus, and how do those two interpretations differ fundamentally?

*What is the strongest point in my position?*

My chosen strategy for this book's debate seems to me the strongest point of its position. I tried to enter inside your alleged apocalyptic continuum from the Baptist to Mark and ask what distinctions you would have to make to explain what actually happened across the first century. Granted that "Christianity" did not slowly falter and eventually fail, what options were present within its apocalypticism that allowed steady growth and ultimate success? What changes had to be made and how did they develop? As long as non-apocalypticists argue their position, apocalypticists need not explore the divergent modes, options, and contents of that claimed apocalyptic continuum. It is my considered judgment but also, of course, my utterly partial conclusion that you have not faced, let alone answered, my present mode of internal argumentation. Those multiple distinctions, however better they might be articulated in the future, still stand as the strongest point that I see in my own present position in this book. They demand detailed response. For example, how exactly did some of those earliest Christians drop or change the future imminence of apocalyptic consummation (actually, the past commencement of apocalyptic consummation) and yet hold on firmly to Jesus' resurrection as the start of the general resurrection? If you are wrong on apocalypse, are you not also wrong on resurrection?

*What is the weakest point in the other position?*

I find two general items under this rubric, one general and one very specific. The general weakness is the Schweitzer Paradox: how does one get an imperious command out of a mistaken opinion? or the Allison Paradox: how does one get the only dream worth dreaming out of a wrong and irrational position? I remind you, once again, Dale, of these two quotations (1) "Surely if Jesus was, as so many have held, an eschatological prophet who lived in the imaginative world of the apocalypses, we should not expect much consistency from him, for the *essential irrationality* of apocalyptic is manifest from the history of messianic and millenarian movements."[15] (2) "Jesus the millenarian prophet, like all millenarian prophets, was *wrong*: reality has taken no notice of his imagination. . . . And yet, despite everything, for those who have ears to hear, Jesus, the millenarian herald of judgment and salvation, says the only things worth saying, for *his dream is the only one worth dreaming*."[16] *If* you are correct about Jesus as wrong and irrational, you must explain how such origins were transmuted into a credible world religion which still insisted on a basis in Jesus' resurrection as the start of the general resurrection. It not only remained within an apocalyptic framework but insisted that the very consummation of that scenario had already begun, not that the start of the end was near but that the end of the end had begun.

The very specific weakness is also personal for me. As mentioned above, and with references, I have insisted across my entire professional career that Jesus was eschatological but not apocalyptic. But you have repeatedly stated that I maintain a non-eschatological Jesus. For example, from 1994: "the eschatolological Jesus has been put to death? by [among others] John Dominic Crossan,"[17] and, as late as 2000: "Perhaps the most prominent exponent of a noneschatological Jesus today is John Dominic Crossan."[18] But in *Jesus of Nazareth* from 1998 you footnoted that "Crossan's Jesus, for example, is eschatological by his (Crossan's) understanding of 'eschatology' (having to do with a divine utopia, not necessarily the end of the world) but not by mine."[19] That footnote is simply not enough for useful debate. We have both agreed in print that Jesus is announcing heaven on earth. From my *The Historical Jesus* of 1991: "The everlasting Kingdom is apocalyptic, however, not in the sense of a destroyed earth and an evacuation heavenward for the elect, but rather of something like a heaven on earth."[20] From your *Jesus of Nazareth* in 1998: "'Heaven on earth,' we might say."[21] That is where our debate should focus: not on destructive "end of world" but on transformative "heaven on earth" (or divine utopia).

15. Allison, *Jesus*, 4 (italics added).
16. Allison, *Jesus*, 218–19 (italics added).
17. Allison, "Plea," 668.
18. Allison, "Eschatology," 269 (despite its citation of *In Parables* from 1973).
19. Allison, *Jesus*, 34, note 103.
20. Crossan, *Historical Jesus*, 285.
21. Allison, *Jesus*, 156.

*What is the strongest point in the other position?*

I see two very major strengths in your book's position, Dale. The first is your argument for apocalyptic continuity from John the Baptist through Jesus and on into Paul, the Q Gospel, and Mark. Since a definite conceptual connection goes forward from John to Jesus and backward from those other three sources to Jesus, it seems most likely that he himself was not a non-apocalyptic exception in that continuum of apocalypse. My only comment on that argument was to note that while it was circumstantially compelling, it was not logically absolute. Jesus *could* have been a non-apocalyptic island in an apocalyptic sea just as Gandhi was a non-violent island in a violent sea.[22] It would not be the first time that a founder had to struggle against both predecessors and successors, opponents and followers, with a vision too radical for either. That said, however, I think your second and even stronger argument not only stands by itself, it also powerfully supports that former claim.

You are quite correct in your assertion that Jesus makes apocalyptic statements at almost every level and in every genre of the tradition. The texts are there and I agree absolutely on their presence and their meaning. As far as I am concerned, for example, a saying like Mark 9:1 (the kingdom will come in power in the lifetime of the disciples) is apocalyptic. No question and no debate. If I thought Jesus said something like that, I would consider him not just eschatological but apocalyptic.[23]

When that second argument is combined with the first one, the combination is seemingly impregnable. Furthermore, common sense seems to be on its side and that is extremely important in public discourse. When people read or hear the synoptic gospels they find apocalyptic language regularly on the lips of Jesus and it seems to be sheer prejudice to call him non-apocalyptic. If, to keep the argument simple, you argue from Mark 9:1 and I consider that from Mark and not from Jesus, my response sounds absolutely circular (even if you do not so accuse me). I must have decided that apocalypticism was bad, Jesus was not apocalyptic, and any such statements could not derive from Jesus. It sounds like the worst special pleading. How, one might ask, and apart from a priori bias, can anyone argue for a non-apocalyptic

---

22. Allison, *Jesus*, 40, note 119.
23. Allison, *Jesus*, 44, notes 135–138.

Jesus when an apocalyptic Jesus is clearly and obviously present in our texts?

*What is the weakest point in my position?*

If in this book I had argued directly for a non-apocalyptic Jesus, rather than arguing for it indirectly from within your own position, those strengths of yours would have been my worst weaknesses. I would have argued that you had not stratified the texts into their divergent layers asking, for example, what in Mark came from Jesus and what came from Mark himself – especially with regard to apocalypticism. In fact, it seems to me that most of the recent books on the historical Jesus have ignored stratigraphy either programmatically (Tom Wright) or practically (Paula Fredriksen, Bruce Chilton). It is almost as if source-criticism and redaction-criticism can now be noisily or quietly ignored. If, for example, we know what happened among written traditions between 70 and 100 (Mark to John), what do we think was happening among oral traditions from 30 to 70? I would have argued, as I did following Steve Patterson in *The Birth of Christianity*, that the Common Sayings Tradition used independently by the Q Gospel and the Gospel of Thomas was eschatological but neither ascetically nor apocalyptically so. What, therefore, I would have asked, is that third mode of eschatology? I still think that is completely correct, but I consider it almost a lost cause to argue along those lines at the moment. That is one reason, but not the only one, why I argued with you as I did.

In terms of my actual arguments, that is, in terms of the distinctions I proposed as necessitated by your own alleged apocalyptic continuum, I have yet to see their weaknesses. No doubt they are there but I need critical and collegial response to them before being able to see their weaknesses.

# STEPHEN PATTERSON

*What is the strongest point in my position?*

First, let me be clear that I do not regard my position to be superior to Dale's because I consider myself more up-to-date or harder-working than he. The relevant bibliographies (on Matthew, Q, and Jesus, etc.) clearly reveal why Dale's erudition and scholarly productivity are widely respected in our discipline. My comment about "slogging through the muck of historical-critical scholarship" was not meant to imply that Dale's approach was more slothful, but to draw the genuine contrast between Dale's decision to begin with the broad historical strokes represented by his "five pillars" and my decision to begin with detailed historical-critical analysis of texts. Similarly, my comments about working at this in an open forum (yes, the Jesus Seminar) was not to suggest that Dale has worked uncritically as a lone wolf, but simply to say that the discussion of historical-critical matters had forced me to change my mind about many things about Jesus, among them the very issue we are debating now. This was in genuine contrast to Dale, who has asserted that such analysis could never dissuade him from the position suggested to him by his five pillars, a position from which he has now backed away (see above pp. 88–89).

In all of this, the genuine contrast I was attempting to underscore was on the question of where to begin – with broad-stroke historical observations or with detailed analysis of texts and traditions. I have chosen to begin with the latter, and I would identify this as the strength of my position. This decision has its greatest payoff, in my view, in our understanding of the parables tradition. Here critical analysis has for about a century consistently rejected the allegorical interpretation of the parables as secondary. And it is precisely in their allegorical treatment at the hands of the synoptic authors that the parables find their focus in the future apocalyptic judgment that is to come. If they are not elaborate allegories for the coming judgment, what then shall we do with these multivalent, creative images of life lived (now!) under the reign of God? As Bob Miller has recently pointed out, among those recent contributions to the discussion that have emphasized the apocalypticism of Jesus' preaching, the parables of Jesus are conspicuously absent.[24] Indeed, it is difficult to know what to do with the parables, or with the scores of similarly multivalent aphorisms, under the hypothesis of an apocalyptic Jesus.

*What is the weakest point in the other position?*

First let it be said that the weakest aspect of Dale's position is certainly not that he is out of date and out of step with the inevitable progress of scholarship as it strides ever-forward to the

---

24. Miller, "Apocalyptic Jesus", 113–14.

truth. If I implied this in my response to Dale by calling attention to Dale's dismissal of Kloppenborg's work, that was a careless thing to do. Dale certainly deserves to be credited for his own substantial contribution to Q studies, and for maintaining a healthy skepticism over against the theories of Kloppenborg, Lührmann, Jacobson, and others who see the arrival of apocalyptic material in the Q tradition as relatively late, or "redactional." Indeed, my own appeal to the New Questers – Käsemann, Conzelmann, and Vielhauer – who first broke with Schweitzer's apocalyptic hypothesis in the 1950s and 60s, could be seen as a little out of date. One person's progress is another's regress, to be sure.

Nevertheless, the weakness of Dale's position, in my view, is the failure of his position adequately to account for the diversity of early Christianity, as many have come to see it today. Of course, this is a development in New Testament scholarship that I would credit as a genuine advance, while Dale and others might not. Indeed, in emphasizing the widespread nature of apocalypticism in early Christianity – even suggesting in the present volume that the Gospel of John embraces an apocalyptic eschatology – Dale seems to see things as a little more monolithic than I do. Nonetheless, I regard this appreciation of early Christian diversity as a real step forward in scholarship, owing to the greater attention paid today to texts like the Gospel of Thomas, or to historical matters, such as the theological position of Paul's various opponents.

Given the theological diversity of early Christian texts and traditions, it is compelling to me that sapiential material is present in virtually every domain of the Jesus tradition, even though it dominates in none of them. How can we account for this sapiential substratum lying beneath the apocalypticism of Mark and the synoptics, the Christianized strains of Hellenistic Judaism in John, and the incipient Gnosticism of Thomas? And what should we make of Paul's opponents in First Corinthians, who seek Wisdom in spiritual ecstasy and say "There is no resurrection of the dead," thus denying the linchpin of Paul's apocalyptic perspective? History, of course, can be complicated. But the simplest scenario suggested by all of this diversity laid atop a sapiential base is the one I have proposed: Jesus preached a kind of counter-cultural wisdom, from which various interpretive branches emerged, among them, apocalyptic. If, on the other hand, one posits an apocalyptic point of origin, this diversity is more difficult to explain. Moreover, the ubiquitous presence of sapiential materials becomes an anomaly not easily accounted for. It is possible, of course, that those who cultivated the Thomas tradition had before them the apocalyptic sayings and parables of Jesus, systematically removed their apocalyptic elements, and then added in a new Gnostic twist to some, while saving others as simple wisdom forms. But this seems more complicated, leaving more loose ends than is necessary.

*What is the strongest point in the other position?*

The strength of Dale's position stands out over against the weakest aspect of my own. His understanding of apocalyptic is subtle and nuanced. That Jesus could have entertained an aphoristic imagination even while anticipating the imminent end of civilization is probably true. As Dale points out, it is not necessary that Jesus be utterly consistent as a thinker in order to remain plausible as a figure of history. To the contrary, perhaps a less than consistent Jesus is by far the more plausible. In parsing out the differing perspectives of wisdom and apocalyptic, we who differ with Dale may be creating a choice that a real person of antiquity might not feel compelled to make. If consistency is the hobgoblin of small minds, one could in fact argue that Jesus most plausibly would not have been very consistent.

I am most troubled by the question of consistency when I consider the relationship between John the Baptist and Jesus. As Marc has pointed out, if Jesus was originally a follower of John the Baptist, then he obviously would have originally shared John's apocalyptic viewpoint (if indeed this is an apt description of John's preaching). I have argued, following the likes of Käsemann, that when Jesus left the circle of the Baptist it was quite likely because his point of view had changed, particularly on the issue of whether the Empire of God was still to come, or, was already (potentially) present. But even if this was so, how decisively would he have changed his mind? And what of those who may have gone out with Jesus (as John 1:35ff. avers), who also had heard the Baptist, but decided ultimately for Jesus? Can one reasonably imagine that as Jesus carried on away from John's circle that this question never arose again? Can one reasonably assume that those who went with Jesus would never have had second thoughts, or argued with Jesus over this issue, or that Jesus himself never had second thoughts? And finally, what conversations might have taken place after Jesus was killed? What sort of doubts and second thoughts would this second catastrophe have triggered among the followers of both John and Jesus? It is no wonder that the Jesus tradition contains both apocalyptic and anti-apocalyptic strains. The question is, did these competing claims arise in the aftermath of Jesus' death, as his followers struggled to find meaning in the wake of their whole experience with him, including his roots in the Baptist's following, or did they arise already in the preaching of Jesus himself, as he struggled with his own Baptist roots? Dale has criticized Marc for entertaining the notion of a Jesus with evolving views, but here that old hobgoblin of consistency makes his appearance again. A real Jesus might easily have changed his mind on the nature of the Empire of God, even more than once.

*I would feel more secure in my position if . . .*

We had decent sources with which to work! If we only had something in writing from Jesus himself! Or, failing that, if we could at least have something from John the Baptist! Lacking these crucial pieces of evidence we will always be confined to the sort of speculation with which we have simply grown comfortable. Sometimes the effort of scholarship, our familiarity with sources and with secondary literature, or with any of the various helpful fields in which one can establish some level of expertise, all of this effort and demonstrated competence can lead us to believe that we really have a firm grip on Jesus after all. But at the end of the day, beneath this show of effort, there is finally the scanty evidence on which we must all in some way rely. And it is scanty, sketchy, and subject to numerous and varied interpretations.

This does not mean that we should give up on the task, as so many have argued before. I trust we will all agree on that. The stakes are too high to give up completely. But the high stakes this conversation involves should not pressure us into claiming more for our efforts than they can reasonably bear. This dialogue is reminding me of that once again. Dale makes sense of what he sees. Other things catch my gaze, and so I go a different way. As we argue over what to look at, and how to understand what we are seeing, "probably," "perhaps," and "maybe" will have to do for now.

# Part 3:
# So What?

# The Historical Jesus and Early Christianity

Marcus Borg
John Dominic Crossan
Stephen Patterson

This chapter explores the implications that reconstructions of the historical Jesus have for how we understand early Christianity. Here the contributors discuss how their understanding of Jesus helps them to make better sense of the historical data for first-century Christianity. They approach this discussion by answering two related questions, one positive and one negative. First, what is there about early Christianity that your hypothesis about the historical Jesus makes it easier to understand? Second, what is there about early Christianity that the opposite hypothesis makes it more difficult to understand?

*Editor's Note:* Dale Allison's argument that Jesus was an apocalyptic prophet is based squarely on his interpretation of first-century Christianity. He builds his case for adopting the paradigm that Jesus was a millenarian prophet on five "pillars," four of which are fashioned directly out of data from early Christianity (see above, pp. 20–24 and 84–89). In other words, Dale is led to consider Jesus an apocalyptic figure in large part because that makes it easier for him to understand why early Christianity developed the way it did. In light of this Dale decided, and the editor agreed, that it would be redundant for him to rehash those arguments in this chapter.

## MARCUS BORG

I will address two questions in this chapter. (1) What is there about early Christianity that the hypothesis of a non-apocalyptic Jesus makes it easier to understand? (2) What is there about early Christianity that the hypothesis of an apocalyptic Jesus makes it

131

more difficult to understand? Because they are two sides of the same coin, I will treat them together.

I emphasize that I will be citing difficulties that go with seeing Jesus through the paradigm of *primary* apocalyptic eschatology. If apocalyptic eschatology is affirmed but seen as secondary, the problems become far less difficult and perhaps even disappear. But given that Dale is arguing for apocalyptic eschatology as a paradigm, it seems to me that his position does face the following difficulties.

I will describe four features of early Christianity that are more easily understood within the paradigm of a non-apocalyptic historical Jesus, and more difficult to understand within the paradigm of an apocalyptic historical Jesus. My claim is that my understanding of Jesus makes it easier to understand what we know of early Christianity than Dale's does.

1. If apocalyptic eschatology had been primary for Jesus and for early Christianity, I would expect to see more traces in early Christianity of a crisis of confidence about the delay of the apocalyptic consummation. There is relatively little evidence in the New Testament and in second and third-century Christianity that unfulfilled apocalyptic expectation was a major crisis.

There is, of course, 2 Pet 3:3–10. Dated by most scholars in the early second century, it refers to "scoffers" who ask, "Where is the promise of Jesus' coming?" It rebuts the scoffers by affirming that "with the Lord one day is like a thousand years, and a thousand years are like one day," and that the delay is to give people more time for repentance.

The other piece of evidence sometimes cited is based on Hans Conzelmann's analysis of Luke-Acts. Some fifty years ago, Conzelmann argued that Luke modified the imminent apocalyptic expectation found in Mark and Matthew so that Jesus became "the middle of time" rather than the one who brought the end of time. But an alternative case is also plausible. As I suggested in an earlier chapter, both Mark and Matthew reflect heightened apocalyptic expectation generated by the crises of the 40s and 60s, and it is this expectation that Luke counters. Rather than correcting an apocalyptic expectation that originated with Jesus, Luke is affirming the original non-apocalyptic message of Jesus against the mistaken notion arising out of the crises of the 40s and 60s, that the apocalypse was at hand. But whether one thinks

Conzelmann's case or the alternative to be more plausible, there is not much evidence that early Christianity faced a crisis because of apocalyptic disappointment.

2. A major theme of the gospels and Paul is "the way" as "following Jesus." It is central to Mark. Though Mark has an apocalyptic eschatology, it plays a surprisingly minor role in his presentation of Jesus. Rather, his gospel as a whole is about "the way" or "the path," and the way is following Jesus. In the great central section of Mark (8:27–10:45), the theme of discipleship is understood as following Jesus. Three times in this section, the Jesus of Mark speaks of his impending death and resurrection in Jerusalem. To follow Jesus means to follow him on the way that leads to Jerusalem, the place of death and resurrection, of endings and new beginnings. Discipleship means to follow Jesus on the path of death; Jesus' death thus became a metaphor for the path of following him. Both Matthew and Luke incorporate this understanding into their gospels. For them, as for Mark, following the way of Jesus is a central image for the Christian life.

So also in Paul. By no later than the early 50s, Paul was already speaking of the death and resurrection of Jesus as a metaphor for the internal path of personal transformation. Of course, for Paul (as for the synoptic authors), the death and resurrection of Jesus was more than a metaphor for internal transformation; as Paul tells us, "I have seen the Lord" (1 Cor 9:1). Nevertheless, Paul also uses Jesus' death and resurrection as a metaphor for internal transformation, most clearly in Galatians 2 and Romans 6. In Gal 2:19–20, Paul writes, "I have been crucified with Christ; and it is no longer I who live, but Christ who lives in me."

Paul understands following the path of Jesus to mean dying to an old identity and way of being, and being born into a new identity and way of being. An emphasis on "the way" is also central to John and Acts. In the Gospel of John, Jesus is "the way." That is, in Jesus, we see what "the way" looks like embodied in a human life. In Acts, the earliest name of the early Christian movement is "the Way."

This early and widespread emphasis on "the way" as "following Jesus" does not fit the paradigm of primary apocalyptic very well. What could it mean to follow the path of a millenarian prophet who believed passionately but wrongly that God would soon intervene dramatically to transform the world, including such history-ending events as the resurrection of the dead and the last judgment? Would it mean primarily to continue the proclamation that the transformation is near? To continue to hope? And does this really do justice to following Jesus as following *a way*?

Moreover, the content of what it means to follow Jesus (namely, dying to an old identity and way of being) has little to do with millenarian expectation. How do we get from "millenarian prophet" to what we see in the gospels and Paul about the way of Jesus? How does one account for this remarkable symmetry? Are we to think that Paul and Mark and John independently spiritualized the apocalyptic eschatology of Jesus into a path of internal transformation? What connection between these two notions can we imagine? In my judgment, it is more plausible to see the metaphor of "the way," so central to Paul and the gospels, as grounded in Jesus' own wisdom teaching. To sum up this point: why this focus on "the way" in early Christianity? To me, it seems obvious: because Jesus as a wisdom teacher taught this way. Like the Buddha, he taught a way or path of internal transformation that flowed out of his own experience of the sacred. After his death, his followers saw the way that Jesus had taught also embodied in his death and resurrection.

Dale could, of course, agree with this claim and still argue that Jesus expected the apocalypse. But the more that Dale integrates elements like "wisdom teacher of a way" into his understanding of Jesus, and "the way" as a major theme of early Christianity, the less apt "millenarian prophet" becomes as a shorthand characterization of Jesus. Apocalyptic eschatology would become one element in a sketch of Jesus, rather than the paradigm through which to see his mission and teaching. To use one of his own examples, Dale notes that Martin Luther had some millenarian expectations. Dale's point is that millenarian belief can be combined with non-millenarian passion. My point is different: granted that Luther had such beliefs, would we then think that "millenarian prophet" would be a good shorthand characterization of Luther? No. To risk belaboring the point, we would say, "Luther was primarily a reformer who also had millenarian beliefs."

3. What we can see of the "shape" of early Christian life does not fit well with the hypothesis that millenarian prophet is the best paradigm for understanding Jesus. The emphasis of early Christian preaching and teaching seems to have been on present

transformation, not on preparing for God's apocalyptic act. Paul was far more concerned to affirm that the new age had begun than to proclaim, "You'd better be ready, because the last judgment is coming soon." His message does not seem to have been, "God's going to fix everything soon, and you'd better be on the right side when that happens," but "The transformation has begun: you can be part of it; come along with us."

So also with the centrality of meal practice – of eating together – in early Christianity. Was the emphasis on shared meals central because they thought the apocalyptic banquet was at hand? Or did they make eating together central because it was central to the vision and practice of Jesus, even as many of them also thought that the consummation was near? At issue, once again, is whether apocalyptic expectation is seen as primary or secondary. The more it is made primary, the less able we are to understand Jesus and early Christianity. The more it is made secondary, the less appropriate it becomes to refer to it as a paradigm.

4. I think my understanding of Jesus makes it easier to understand the development of christology than does Dale's. Relatively soon after the death of Jesus, his followers began to speak of him as a divine reality. He was now "one with God" and "at the right hand of God." Prayers and praise were addressed to him as if to God. I do not know how soon one of them simply equated Jesus with God by saying, "Jesus *is* God." The expression does not occur in the New Testament itself, though it is in use by around 115 C.E. when the Christian bishop and martyr Ignatius referred to "our God Jesus." But it is nevertheless clear that the post-Easter Jesus became the functional equivalent of God soon after his death. This is especially remarkable because his followers were also Jewish monotheists.

That Jesus was a millenarian prophet makes it difficult to understand this development. Why would they conclude that a mistaken millenarian prophet was "one with God," a divine reality to whom prayer and praise could be addressed as if to God?

And why, if Jesus were a millenarian prophet whose mistake became more obvious over time, would the community's christology become stronger and higher over time?

My understanding of Jesus offers a more plausible account of early Christian christological development. In addition to seeing Jesus as a healer, wisdom teacher, movement founder and social prophet, I emphasize that he was a Jewish mystic. A mystic like Jesus is a Spirit-filled person. I think it likely that the followers of Jesus even during his historical lifetime sometimes experienced the presence of the Spirit in or around him. I do not think they experienced him as "ordinary." Thus I think his followers had a sense already during his lifetime of the Spirit of God being present in Jesus to a remarkable degree. Of course, this wasn't apparent to everybody. Critics could conclude that it was an evil spirit that was present in him. Nevertheless, I think there was sometimes a whiff of the numinous around him.

Thus I see the community's christology grounded in part in what they had experienced of the historical Jesus. At least equally important is the community's post-Easter experience of Jesus. Soon after his death, some of his followers experienced him as a divine reality. Easter, as I have mentioned before, is not simply about the survival of death, but is about the experience and affirmation of Jesus as "Lord." The one whom they had known as a Spirit-filled healer, wisdom teacher, movement founder and social prophet was now at God's right hand, and the Spirit they had known in him had now come upon the community and continued to be present within the community. No wonder they began to speak of him with the most exalted language they knew: as the Word and Wisdom of God, as the only-begotten Son of God, as Lord and Christ, as the lamb of God, the light of the world, the bread of life, the way, the truth, and the life.

Of course, I do not know that it happened this way. The previous paragraphs include considerable speculation. But I do think that my scenario is more plausible than one that begins with Jesus as a millenarian prophet. It is, of course, *possible* to imagine a scenario that leads from millenarian prophet to the remarkable christological affirmations made by the early Christians. But historical arguments are not simply about possibility, but about plausibility and probability. In my judgment, it is difficult to get from millenarian prophet to the richly varied and highly exalted christological metaphors of the New Testament. The development seems unlikely. And if it did happen, it also seems wrong. Is it not a mistake, or at least misleading, to speak of a mistaken millenarian prophet as the Word and Wisdom of God?

As I end my contribution to this chapter, I want to emphasize once again that these are difficulties associated with the paradigm of *primary* apocalyptic eschatology. When it becomes the paradigm for seeing Jesus, it is difficult to see much continuity between what Jesus was like and the developments that we see in early Christianity. On the other hand, a non-apocalyptic paradigm (or a paradigm in which apocalyptic is secondary) enables us to see considerable continuity between Jesus and his first-century followers.

# JOHN DOMINIC CROSSAN

The expression "end of the world" blocks us almost inevitably from understanding what was at stake for first-century Jews and Christians in announcing the imminence or presence of apocalyptic consummation. A chasm yawns between us and them, present and past, moderns and ancients, and it derives from two facts. One is that we can realistically imagine *ourselves* destroying human life definitely, all life probably, and even our planet possibly. And we can do some or all of that chemically and/or biologically and/or atomically. Another is that, apart from what can now be done *by* us, we can imagine cosmic accidents such as giant meteorites doing much the same *to* us.

## "End of the World" as Transcendental Red Herring

When, then, we hear about "the end of the world" in first-century texts it is almost impossible for our twenty-first century minds not to think of it as primarily if not exclusively a destructive phenomenon. And, therefore, since no such terrestrial destruction has ever happened, its imminent announcement has always been "wrong" and its continued announcement may even be called "irrational." But for ancient Jews and Christians, such destruction could be effected only by divine power and that would not happen unless God annulled creation and the covenant made inaugurally with earth. God saw that the world was good then but it is not so any longer? But that could never be. Cosmic transformation, therefore, but never cosmic destruction.

Dale made this point about cross-cultural millenarianism in general:

> Hope casts itself not upon an otherworldly afterlife but longs for [as Yonina Talmon says] "the metahistorical future in which the world will be inhabited by a humanity liberated from all limitations of human existence, redeemed from pain and transience, from fallibility

and sin, thus becoming at once perfectly good and perfectly happy. The world will be utterly, completely and irrevocably changed."[1]

Dale also applied that generality to the historical Jesus in particular:

> [M]ost millenarian movements, whether ancient, medieval, or modern, have expected not the utter destruction and replacement of this world but rather a revolutionary change . . . [M]aybe the best conclusion with regard to Jesus is that the difference between heaven and earth became, in his imagination, indistinct in the eschaton, that is, the two things in effect merged and became one. "Heaven on earth," we might say.[2]

You will recall that, in my first response to Dale above, I noted that each of us had used that phrase "heaven on earth" for the historical Jesus. On earth, as in heaven. Not, in heaven instead of earth.

In other words, I think that Dale Allison and I agree (as probably do most other scholars) that apocalyptic eschatology wastransformative rather than destructive. It did not imagine the "end of this world" as a place-time physical reality but the end of this world as a place-time material location of dearth and disease, labor and hardship, as well as a place-time moral location of evil and impurity, war and violence, inequity and injustice. Maybe, then, we should retire forever that now-misleading phrase "end of the world" and speak, as the ancients intended, about "the end of the present aeon of evil." That would insist that, however unimaginably transformed such an after-world would be, it would all happen down here in a (e)utopian world, down here on a perfected earth. None of that intends to protect apocalypticists from error but rather to protect us from inaccuracy. We are guilty of historical malpractice to go on using a phrase that can only misunderstand the past and mislead the present. *A millenarian seer or apocalyptic prophet announces the imminent transcendental change of a terribly evil world into a perfectly good one.* Say that clearly, and we might get somewhere. At least we might get to something worth arguing about. Go on talking about "the end of the world" and only misunderstanding and irrelevance are possible.

1. Allison, *Jesus*, 85.
2. Allison, *Jesus*, 155–56.

Once that is said clearly and emphasized repeatedly, all sorts of sub-questions may be faced. What, in the first place, are the precise dimensions of that evil so serious that it demands a transcendental solution? Why, for example, should we imagine that all those involved in apocalyptic expectation would agree on the contents and priorities of that consummation? Why would women and men, slaves and free, illiterate and literate, poor and rich, peasant and aristocrats agree on those details? What, in the second place, are the precise elements in the proposed transcendental solution, be it from angels or ancestors, gods, goddesses, or God? All would agree, no doubt, as long as transcendental problems and transcendental solutions were phrased in the language of parable, myth, or hyperbole. But, even there, difficulties could arise. Recall that citation from Sibylline Oracles 2 which I used earlier in my first response:

> The earth will belong equally to all, undivided by walls or fences. . . .
> Lives will be in common and wealth will have no division.
> For there will be no poor man there, no rich, and no tyrant, no slave.
> Further, no one will be either great or small.

Even as eschatological apocalypticism, would aristocratic rulers agree with the content of that future hope? Some might agree, to return to an earlier example, that the pagans would convert to God at the end-time of evil. But what if somebody asked about the details, about the ways and means of that event? All might agree, to take another example, with the apocalyptic "return of the lost tribes." But what if someone got into housing arrangements? The mono-apocalypticism that lurks behind the debate on Jesus as pro or anti-apocalyptic needs to be discussed more fully before that latter question can be usefully faced.

## The Problem of Literal and/or Metaphorical Language

What was at stake for those early Christian apocalypticists is quite clear in general terms. If they spoke only of *imminence*, they hoped that God in Christ would soon create a world of perfect holiness here below. If they spoke of *presence*, they believed that God in Christ had already begun to do so. I have insisted in my earlier responses, and continue to do so here, that at least all those who professed resurrectional faith, had to operate under that latter rubric. And, furthermore, that they presumed not only the start but the end of the apocalyptic scenario to have begun with Jesus' resurrection. You will recall, that *for the present debate*, I simply accept Dale's thesis of apocalyptic continuity from John the Baptist to Mark and emphasize that their insistence on the resurrection of Jesus makes any withdrawal from that apocalypticism impossible. I repeat: apocalypticism and resurrection stand or fall together. From all of that, I get this major problem. What, on earth (pun intended), did they experience themselves that made such a claim possible and what did they explain to others that made it credible? It is that question which brings me back to what I avoided earlier: the problem of literal and/or metaphorical language in cross-cultural, Jewish, or Christian apocalypticism.

One crucial point before proceeding. Metaphor must be metaphorical of *something*. To use metaphor is to point to that *something*. When and if apocalyptic language is metaphorical, there must still be *something* to which it refers. And, then, the question becomes this: what is that *something*? You had suggested that apocalyptic language should be taken literally.[3] Only this section in your entire book made what I considered two cheap cracks[4] and I wondered if you were just being "therapeutically provocative" with that part of your thesis. You responded with two points. One was that you "stressed the literal nature of apocalyptic forecasts because Tom Wright stresses instead their metaphorical nature" and you were "unconvinced that whoever first composed future Son of man sayings would have agreed with Tom that they were fulfilled in the destruction of Jerusalem in 70 c.e."[5]

I agree with you against Tom there. But he could have the wrong *something*, the wrong referent for metaphorical language, and it still not be literal language. Your other point was this:

> The eschatological vision of the early Jesus tradition is a vision of utopia, and utopia has not come. So my case for literalism was an attempt to resist correlating Jesus' eschatological vision with anything history has had to offer. I was not trying to unfold the essence of apocalyptic eschatology, which for me is a transcendent and universal solution to the problem of evil.[6]

---

3. See Allison, *Jesus*, 152–69.
4. See Allison, *Jesus*, 164, 166.
5. Above, p. 100.
6. Above, pp. 100–101.

How do you, or I, decide that "utopia has not come," especially when confronted with people who assert that it has?
Confronted, I repeat, not just with people who say it is imminent
but with people who announce its climactic presence? They are
clearly claiming what you correctly describe as "a transcendent
and universal solution to the problem of evil," but why should
certain people at a certain place and time not find that transcendence incarnated in their experience and their lives? All of that
metaphorical or hyperbolic language must have become experien-
tially present for those who announced it credibly to themselves
and to some others as well.

I asked you, almost in passing, what you thought, for example,
about the eschatology of Virgil's *Fourth Eclogue*. I ask it again, as
an example of a pagan rather than a Jewish or Christian apocalypse. If he had been interviewed on his death-bed in 19 B.C.E.,
would Virgil have claimed what Augustus did for Rome in general
and for himself in particular to be an adequate *something* for that
poem's metaphorico-hyperbolic language. Was the *Pax Romana*
an appropriate referent for that ram in the meadow changing his
fleece regularly "now to sweetly blushing purple, now to a saffron
yellow" so that "of its own will shall scarlet clothe the grazing
lambs." If you argued that Virgil took that literally, I would be
unable to prove the opposite. My problem is not that it was all
too long ago or that the ancients are inscrutable to me. I have
exactly the same problem with moderns. I have not the faintest
idea how my contemporaries think about witches after seeing the
*Blair Witch Project*, about ghosts after seeing *The Sixth Sense*, or
about miracles and prophecies after reading the tabloids in passing through the check-out lanes with groceries. I presume, actually, that *both* ancients *and* moderns took such matters on a
spectrum from 100% literal to 100% metaphorical and at all possible points in between. Most probably, therefore, *some* ancients
and *some* moderns, would have taken all apocalyptic language literally. Some, likewise, metaphorically. But, I repeat, it had to be
metaphorical of *something* demonstrably present for *somebody* to
experience.

How, in conclusion, would Paul have argued his faith to a nice,
polite pagan colleague as they worked together in a leather shop?
What was the something that convinced him a new creation was
all around them, not just imminent but present. What would have
been at stake for him in such a conversation? This? God, that is, a

God of distributive justice and not just of absolute power, has begun the climactic justification of the world by raising Jesus from the dead and thereby negating the official, legal, and public power of imperial Rome. But where and how, Paul, is that at work? What could Paul answer? Something like this? There is a small group of us who meet for prayer in a shop near here before it opens each day. And once a week we meet there to share half of all we have from the preceding week's work. We call that meal the Lord's Supper because we believe that all creation belongs to the Lord and that we must share the Lord's food equally among us. We share what is not our own, that is the Lord's type of meal, the Lord's style of supper. So, I invite you. Come and see if God is not already making a more perfect world right under your very nose. And, by the way, we have small groups like the one here in every city of the Roman Empire. It is not just how many we are but how everywhere we are. And whenever one of you turns from Caesar, who crucified Jesus, to God who raised Jesus, you participate in this justification of the world. It is a choice between the divine Caesar and the divine Jesus. Come to the sardine-seller's shop the day after tomorrow to see and decide for yourself. (But come on, Dominic, that is not enough. Enough for whom, Dale?)

# STEPHEN PATTERSON

What is more difficult for me to understand about early Christianity if Jesus was an apocalyptic prophet? What is more easily explained under my hypothesis that Jesus was a prophet of Wisdom?

## Diversity in Early Christianity

The question of how we understand Jesus is closely tied to the question of how we understand earliest Christianity. Our view of Jesus ought in some way help us to explain what we are seeing in the earliest Christian sources, which Dale calls the "early Jesus tradition."

For many years Christians looking back on the origins of their faith have tended to see a singular dominant tradition, traceable back through the centuries, into the earliest (apostolic) sources, and ultimately to Jesus himself. Difference, to the extent that it was noticed, was understood as departure, a branching off from the main (more legitimate) stream of tradition. There was orthodoxy and there was heresy. Orthodoxy began with Jesus, was preserved in the New Testament, articulated in the Apostles' and Nicene Creeds, and safeguarded through the teachings of the church. Part of this orthodox picture, of course, was (and still is) "from thence he shall come to judge the quick and the dead": the apocalyptic final chapter in the synoptic story of Jesus.

Over the past 50 years, however, critical scholarship beginning with Walter Bauer in the 1930s, and then with Helmut Koester and James M. Robinson in the 1960s and 70s, has effectively challenged this simple, if comforting view of early Christianity. The earliest Jesus tradition is not homogeneous. Rather, it is marked by a variety of attempts to find meaning in the words and ministry of Jesus. Early Christians drew on several theological traditions, not just apocalypticism, to express what Jesus had come to mean to them. It is this diversity in the earliest Jesus tradition that is more difficult to understand under Dale's hypothesis.

Of course, it is not diversity itself that is the problem. It is the specific details of the diverse landscape of the early Jesus tradition that are more difficult to understand if Jesus was indeed an apocalyptic prophet. To see this, a brief description of what the sources present us with might be helpful.

## The Specific Diversity of the Early Jesus Tradition

First, the Jesus tradition is replete with material cast in a wisdom form: proverbs, aphorisms, parables, beatitudes, etc. Moreover, these materials have been gathered into sayings collections, a literary form associated with wisdom. This indicates one stream of early thinking about Jesus: he was a sage, or a prophet of Wisdom. He talked about God's will for humankind and how to live more justly and wisely.

Second, the Jesus tradition is marked in many places by apocalypticism. This indicates a second stream of early thinking about Jesus: he was a prophet of the end time. He talked about how the world will end and how to be saved from the wrath to come.

Third, the tradition often portrays Jesus as a messenger from heaven, who has come down to earth to speak of its evils. His mission fulfilled, he returned to heaven, and bids his followers to follow him there when they too shall pass from this earth. He talked about his identity as the descending/ascending redeemer, about the evil world, and about how to achieve heavenly salvation.

These streams are easily harmonized in most Christians' thinking about Jesus, as they frequently were in the early Christian sources themselves. But they are different. The difference between them might be illustrated by imagining how that central concept in Jesus' preaching, the Empire of God, might be conceived in each. Did Jesus speak of the Empire of God as potentially present in the world, as people begin to live in accord with God's wisdom and justice? Or did he speak of a future Empire of God that would begin on earth only after the present world order is destroyed by God's agents, including Jesus, who will be transformed into the fearsome Son of Man wielding the instruments of God's wrath? Or did he speak of an other-worldly, heavenly Empire of God, to which his followers will travel when they die? However cleverly we might harmonize these alternatives, they are in fact very different ways of thinking about Jesus, God, and the world.

Each of these Christian traditions has Jewish precedent and all are equally at home in the world of early Christianity, but they are spread through the Christian sources unevenly. The idea that Jesus was the descending/ascending redeemer sent into the world by God is concentrated in the Gospel of John and the Gospel of Thomas. One does not find it very much in the synoptic sources. On the other hand, the apocalyptic notion of Jesus as the Son of Man, who will return one day to judge all, is concentrated in the synoptic tradition. It is not found in John or Thomas. Finally, there is the aphoristic wisdom tradition. It was not the dominant tradition anywhere, but it is materially present in the synoptic tradition, Thomas, and to an extent, the Gospel of John. One might say that it forms part of the subsoil of each of these traditions.

## Jesus and the Diversity of Early Christianity

Before Bauer, scholars tended to look at this material and ask which of these traditions represents the main stream, the orthodox branch, from which the others diverged as heresy. Their assumption might have been that the truth of Christianity must have been singular, always so, and this singular truth must stem ultimately from Jesus. With the recognition that early Christianity was diverse from its earliest days, a different kind of question emerges. The question is not "Which of these streams is the most legitimate?" but "How can we reconstruct a plausible historical scenario to account for this diversity of interpretation?"

The proposal that Jesus was an apocalyptic prophet does not tally well with the diverse picture I have just described. If Jesus' message was an apocalyptic one, how can we account for the absence of apocalypticism in so much of the tradition? Were Johannine and Thomasine Christianity so out of touch with the character of Jesus' preaching as to miss its main point entirely? And in the synoptic tradition, where the apocalyptic strain is so strong, how can we account for such an extensive subsoil of aphoristic wisdom? If one believes that the world is about to end, how relevant is the question of realizing God's reign in the world through wise and just living? One could argue that wisdom materials were later added to the apocalyptic preaching of Jesus, as a way of grounding salvation in an ethical imperative. But when we examine specific pieces of the tradition, we find no evidence for movement in this direction. On the contrary, in the case of Jesus' parables (a wisdom form) we can see very clearly that many of them have been secondarily pressed in an apocalyptic direction through the technique of allegorization. Here there is clearly development, but not from apocalyptic to wisdom. Rather, the tradition has moved from a wisdom orientation to an apocalyptic one.

How then can we account for the specific pattern of diversity we see in the earliest Jesus tradition? The widespread presence of wisdom materials and forms throughout the tradition suggests that Jesus and his followers were thinking in wisdom categories. To be sure, their wisdom was peculiar – what many have called counter-cultural wisdom – but it is wisdom nonetheless. Their talk must have been about how to live wisely and justly in response to God's will. It is likely that this talk and activity was often focused around the concept of God's Empire (the kingdom of God), a wisdom theme.

But the movement must also have been complex. If it started as a spin-off from John the Baptist's movement, certainly apocalyptic ideas would have been in the air. The argument over whether the new Empire is present now or lies yet in the future may well have raged on among Jesus and his first followers as they themselves struggled to come to grips with John and his ultimate fate. This may be the origin of such sayings as Luke 17:20–21, and its parallels in Thomas 3 and 113.

And what about the descending/ascending redeemer myth: how did this way of thinking get into the mix? On the one hand, some forms of early Jewish Wisdom theology had already incorporated this myth, as is shown by Philo's writings, for example. It is therefore not a giant leap from the sort of aphoristic wisdom one finds throughout the Jesus tradition to the more speculative strains one hears, say, in Jesus' speeches in the Gospel of John. On the other hand, such thinking might also have been present already in the Baptist's movement. Its successors, the Mandaeans, remembered John not as an apocalyptic prophet, but as a descending /ascending redeemer, much like the Jesus who is portrayed in the Gospel of John. In any event, we cannot assume that this way of thinking arose only much later in the Jesus movement. One finds it most unexpectedly, after all, in Q 10:22.

At the risk of oversimplifying the situation, we might then say that Jesus and his first followers were interested in Wisdom theology and its fundamental question: how shall we live wisely and justly in response to God's will. But they thought, argued, and lived in a complex world, full of ideas. Apocalyptic ideas were in the air. So was Wisdom speculation: the idea of a secret and hidden wisdom revealed only to a select few. Jesus certainly knew of these ideas and may have been attracted to them at some point in his life; the same is true of his followers. In the years after Jesus' death, his followers used all of these traditions to give expression to Jesus' significance for their lives. And they combined them with other ideas, such as martyrdom, the noble death, and the resurrection and vindication of fallen heroes, to create a richly complex and diverse tradition.

How legitimate was this? This is, of course, a matter of judgment. But it seems to me that most of this diversity carries within it a certain counter-cultural flavor that has the ring of authenticity. The counter-cultural wisdom of Jesus and his first followers placed them at odds with their culture – the imperial culture of Rome as it was played out in the province of Judaea. Apocalypticism was another way of expressing this dissident attitude; so was Wisdom speculation and its cousin, Gnosticism. Martyrdom and the philosopher's noble death was the appropriate category for understanding his crucifixion. And perhaps the most starkly counter-cultural challenge of all was attaching the central theme of the imperial cult itself – the resurrection, apotheosis, and divinization of the emperor – to Jesus of Nazareth, a peasant crucified for crimes against the state. He spoke, after all, of another Empire, not Rome's Golden Age. The counter-cultural attitude of all this interpretive work has its roots in the counter-cultural wisdom tradition first promulgated by Jesus and his earliest followers.

# The Historical Jesus and Contemporary Faith

Dale Allison
Marcus Borg
John Dominic Crossan
Stephen Patterson

What difference does it make today whether or not Jesus was an apocalyptic prophet? Here our contributors offer their reflections on the implications of their understandings of the historical Jesus for Christian belief and practice today.

## DALE ALLISON

Guiltless, pure, incorruptible, blameless souls went up in a Holocaust of fire, with almighty God nowhere in evidence. What do we need a God for if not to deter the wholesale slaughter of the innocent? I do not care for any of the philosophical and pious reasons and contrived explanations of the rabbis which are mere bromides and clichés. There is and can never be any acceptable excuse for God.
— A Holocaust survivor

If death means extinction, there is no way to make sense of the claim that he [God] loves and cherishes all those who died in the concentration camps, for suffering and death would ultimately triumph over each of those who perished.
— Dan Cohn-Sherbok

I think of myself as an historian, not a theologian, and I like being the former because it's so much easier. Nonetheless, I shall set out what seem to me to be three of the theological correlates of the millenarian Jesus.

1. A Jesus who proclaimed the nearness of the end in the first century must have been a real human being. This is no small point. Docetism may have been condemned long ago as a heresy, but it has never gone away. Much of the popular Christianity I have known seems to think that Jesus was at least three fourths

147

divinity, no more than one quarter human being. If we go back to the ancient church, it wasn't much better. The theologians who confessed Jesus' true humanity balked at the implications. Although Irenaeus, in the second century, could take Matt 24:36 = Mark 13:32 ("Concerning that day and hour, no one knows, neither the angels in heaven nor the Son but only the Father") at face value, other Christians couldn't accept a declaration of Jesus' ignorance. Luke failed to reproduce it. Certain copyists omitted the saying from Matthew. Origen wondered whether Jesus might not be referring to the church of which he is the head. Ambrose attributed "nor the Son" to an Arian interpolation. Athanasius suggested that Jesus only feigned ignorance. The Cappadocians thought that the Son did not know the date on his own but only through the Father; or, as Gregory Nazianzen put it: "He knows as God and knows not as man." Chrysostom, in a prize example of bad exegesis, simply denied that Jesus was ignorant of anything: "neither is the Son ignorant of the day, but is even in full certainty thereof." Here is one point at which the Fathers failed us.

Whether or not Christians today believe that the tradition can heal itself, that it can accommodate the millenarian Jesus by a theory of kenosis or a revised Nestorianism or something else again isn't my concern here. All I wish to stress is that Jesus' eschatological expectations make his humanity not some abstract and irrelevant concession but a glaring, central fact that we can never lay aside and forget.

2. There is another thing that the millenarian Jesus is good for, and it seems to me to be grasped by these words of Albert Schweitzer, which I have long pondered:

> That which is eternal in the words of Jesus is due to the very fact that they are based on an eschatological worldview, and contain the expression of a mind for which the contemporary world with its historical and social circumstances no longer had any existence. They are appropriate, therefore, to any world, for in every world they raise the man who dares to meet their challenge, and does not turn and twist them into meaninglessness, above his world and his time, making him inwardly free, so that he is fitted to be, in his own world and in his own time, a simple channel of the power of Jesus.[1]

1. Schweitzer, *Quest*, 402.

Let me put these sentences beside words of the Jew, Pinchas Lapide, in his commentary on the Sermon on the Mount:

> To aspire to the unattainable is perhaps what is most human in our species. It is certainly the quintessence of Judaism. . . . To Jews a pseudo-realism that accepts the status quo as final and unchangeable seems false. Genuine realism, in contrast, is the restlessness of those thirsting for salvation, the impatience roaring through the Sermon on the Mount .[2]

Both of these quotations help us to understand Jesus. In his imagination, he does not just look forward, from the present to the consummation – he also looks backwards, from the consummation to the present. He engrosses himself in the unadulterated will of God as it will be lived in the kingdom, when Torah will be done on earth as in heaven. Moreover, this ideal will is not for him just a dream about the future but it is equally a demand for the present: eschatology is an imperative. This is one reason he can be so heedless of earthly contingencies, why he is often so radical, and why he always blasts complacency and shallow moralism and disturbs every conscience. Jesus is not primarily concerned with the usual gamut of possibilities but with the unobstructed will of God. He envisages, in the words of Gustavo Gutiérrez, "the utopia that sets history in motion for Christians."[3]

Such an idealistic way of looking at things has its limitations. It's not good for everything, and this is why the history of Christian ethics is the history of qualifying Jesus. At the same time, an eschatological worldview that judges the transient in terms of the transcendent has the great virtue of moving us some distance from, and so giving us much-needed perspective on, the contingencies that we misinterpret as necessities.

There is perhaps an analogy here with the old Christian ascetics. Despite their apparent attempts to seek God in private, they often ended up living very public lives as rural patrons and religious oracles. After they crossed the boundaries of ordinary society by cutting their familial, political, and economic ties, people came to perceive them as impartial judges and they accordingly became personal courts of law and social legislators. Simeon

2. Lapide, *The Sermon on the Mount*, 7.
3. Gutiérrez, *The God of Life*, 120.

Stylites, as a recent commentator has put it, "ran an extensive social service network from the top of his pillar." Jesus was in some ways similar in that his poverty, mild asceticism, and eschatology helped erase the illusions of the status quo and enabled him to proclaim "ought" as opposed to "is." His relaxation of worldly constraints allowed him to live outside of what everybody took for granted and so to imagine new possibilities. His eschatological dream first took him out of this world and then brought him back to confront it. He lived against injustice because he dreamed of its opposite.

3. My final point has to do with the interpretation of Jesus' vision itself, which is more than just ethics. I must begin by reiterating that I've defended a more or less literal understanding of ancient apocalyptic prophecies not because I take them literally, but because I think that the ancients tended to do so. I don't look out my window in the expectation that Jesus will someday come on the clouds and that my eye will see him. For me, eschatology is like protology. None of us was at the beginning, and none of us has yet been to the end, so we see through a glass very darkly: it does not yet appear what things shall be. If we stammer whenever we talk about God, how much more when we talk about the God of the future? Eschatology can be only parables of faith.

What, then, are the meanings of such parables? In Jesus' proclamation they represent a series of implicit confessions. Jesus confesses faith in the righteousness and compassion of Israel's God: God wills that the blind see, the deaf hear, the lame walk, the poor have good news preached to them. Jesus confesses faith in the power of Israel's God: with this God, all things are possible. Jesus confesses faith in the goodness of creation: the God who dresses the lilies of the field will not abandon the world but redeem it, for everything that God has made is very good. Jesus confesses that human beings are of little faith and even evil: God's will is not now done on earth as it is in heaven. And Jesus confesses human inadequacy: if people should pray for the coming of the kingdom, it can be only because the kingdom doesn't come without a transcendent mover.

But it's one thing so to interpret Jesus' vision, quite another to know what to believe for oneself. Millenarian prophets have come and gone, and millenarian movements we always have with us, because justice has always been taken from the weak and the orphan, because the rights of the lowly and the destitute have not been maintained. The meek have never inherited the earth, nor does it seem likely that they ever will. As always, the cries and prayers of the oppressed seem to go up to an indifferent sky. The good and all-powerful God of Jesus hasn't redeemed the world: eschatology isn't realized. So isn't Jesus' vision the dream of a ridiculous man? Doesn't he belong with the desperate cargo cultists my students so callously laugh at?

But I can't laugh at Jesus or the cargo cultists without laughing at myself. For in my heart of hearts I yet hope against hope that our profoundest desires come from God and so ultimately won't be denied. And this means, I take it, that the Creator must win in the end. Now how one should think concretely about such an abstract hope I don't know. But it does seem to me that any divine victory must produce meaning and justice for all, the dead no less than the living. If, at the last, there remain lives empty of meaning, if the weak and needy are never rescued once and for all from the hand of the wicked, then the sort of God I believe in doesn't exist outside the eschatological imagination.

Of course this raises question upon question. If one supposes that something more than the conqueror worm awaits us, does one have in mind a physical resurrection with its insuperable philosophical paradoxes, or the survival of an immaterial soul which so many of the philosophers and neurophysiologists have now decided that we don't have? Can the future really make up for the past, and will God for some unfathomable reason be better to everybody in the future than God has been until now? Doesn't my wish for a happy ending just confirm what Feuerbach and Freud said about Christianity as projection? And isn't belief in the final transcendence of death and history a flight from the world as it is? Doesn't it discourage us from seizing the day, from fighting injustice in the here and now?

These are, however, questions for a lifetime, not for a short book. Further, I don't claim to be Solomon, and I expect to go to my death puzzled about much. Providence has seemingly deigned to leave much in the dark: "Truly you are a God who hides yourself" (Isa 45:15). Yet I expect that, on my death bed, I shall still share Jesus' faith that a good and just God who demands justice for all must be God not of the dead but of the living. In the language of the Eighteen Benedictions, the God who heals the sick, frees captives, and sustains the living with faithfulness is the very same God who will show mercy to the dead and fidelity to those who sleep in the dust. Certainly this was the belief of those early Christians who proclaimed that death didn't have the last word with Jesus.

# MARCUS BORG

I begin by acknowledging the twofold setting of this book: it is a conversation with Steve, Dom and Dale; and it is also written for a larger public. In this chapter, I address primarily that larger public. Steve, Dom and Dale are already familiar with what I will say, not because I have said it to them before, but because the issues are familiar to biblical scholars who have thought about the relationship between their historical scholarship and Christian thought and practice, theology and life.

I will develop three claims. They are in some tension with each other:

1.  Christianity is true independently of arguments made by historians. Neither issues of historical factuality nor historical reconstruction threaten its truth.
2.  Yet Jesus, an historical figure, is utterly central to Christianity.
3.  Thus how we think of Jesus matters. Images of Jesus and images of the Christian life go together.

## The Truth of Christianity

What is at stake in this debate is not the truth of Christianity. Christianity is true independently of particular historical hypotheses about Jesus. It is true regardless of one's conclusion about whether Jesus was a mistaken millenarian prophet.

To clarify: when I affirm that Christianity is true, I do not mean that I see the gospels and the New Testament as historically factual in what they report. The identification of truth with factuality is recent, the product of Western culture since the Enlightenment. It is a modern development (and distortion) that greatly interferes with our ability to hear Scripture as true stories about the divine-human relationship. I see the gospels (and the Bible as a whole) as a mixture of memory and metaphor, of historical memory and metaphorical narrative, and the two are intertwined. The truth of the stories in the gospels (and the Bible) does not depend upon their historical factuality. Thus, for example, I hear the story of Jesus changing water into wine at the wedding in Cana as a true story, even though I don't imagine that it ever happened.

I also mean something more when I say that Christianity is true. I mean that it is true in a functional or pragmatic sense. That is, I mean that Christianity obviously works. The central function of religions is to mediate the sacred. As cultural-linguistic traditions, they create a world in which one lives; their stories and teachings shape one's identity and vision of life; their practices and rituals mediate and internalize the new life of which they speak. Their purpose is the transformation of lives by mediating the sacred.

In this sense, Christianity is manifestly true. With all of its blemishes and in spite of the brutalities committed in its name, Christianity (like any other great religion) works. It mediates the sacred and produces lives of compassion and sometimes saintliness. Hypotheses about the historical Jesus do not affect this.

## The Centrality of Jesus

Yet, to state the obvious, Jesus has enormous significance for Christianity. To crystallize the cumulative meaning of Christianity's christological affirmations: Jesus is for Christians the decisive revelation of God. More specifically, he is the decisive revelation of what can be seen of God in a human life. As the Word of God incarnate, the Wisdom and Spirit of God made flesh, he shows us what a life full of God looks like.

Christianity thus finds the decisive revelation of God in a person. In this respect, it differs from the other major religions. Islam, for example, finds the decisive revelation of God in a book; so also does Judaism, and, for that matter, those forms of Christianity that emphasize an inerrant Bible. I do not think this difference makes Christianity superior. I simply mean that Christianity claims that we find the decisive revelation of God in a person, and not in a book or set of teachings.

Given the centrality of Jesus as the decisive revelation of God, where do we locate that revelation? In the historical Jesus? Or in the canonical Jesus – that is, the Jesus whom we meet on the pages of the New Testament? Did the Word become flesh in Jesus? Or did the Word become primarily words, namely, the words of the canonical narratives? Does Jesus, insofar as we can glimpse him through historical reconstruction, disclose what a life full of God looks like? Or is it only the canonical texts about Jesus that matter? Did the Word become flesh, or did it only become narrative?

Here we come to what has often been a fork in the road for historical Jesus scholars and some theologians. Some affirm that it is only or primarily the historical Jesus who should matter. Others affirm that it is only or primarily the canonical Jesus who should matter. Still others affirm both, and that is my position. I am neither among those who argue for the historical Jesus against the canonical Jesus, nor among those who affirm the canonical Jesus against the historical Jesus. Indeed, I see considerable continuity between the two, and though there is not room to develop this claim, I see that continuity as one of the strengths of my position.

## Images of Jesus and Images of the Christian Life

I return to what is at stake. What is at stake in the question that has generated this book is not the truth of Christianity. What is at stake is more modest but nevertheless important. Specifically at stake is how much of a role the historical study of Jesus can play in shaping Christian life and practice today.

My conclusion that both the canonical Jesus and the historical Jesus matter is based in part on the image of Jesus I think I have found. He strikes me as very relevant to Christian life and practice. But were I to become convinced that Dale's reconstruction of Jesus as a millenarian prophet is correct, I would then give primary emphasis to the canonical Jesus. It seems to me that the paradigm of apocalyptic eschatology makes the historical Jesus largely irrelevant to contemporary Christianity.

Dale's own attempt to state the contemporary significance of Jesus as a millenarian prophet suggests as much. He mentions primarily two points. (1) Jesus' mistaken belief that the apocalyptic act of God was at hand underlines his humanity. (2) The promise of post-apocalypse or post-mortem justice offers rectification of the injustices suffered in this life. That isn't much. We know about Jesus' humanity on other grounds, and the second point suggests that Marx may have been right about Christianity: bear your suffering now, for things will be better in the next world.

My own image of the Christian life has its source in part in what I have glimpsed of the historical Jesus. But that is not its only source. Though I was raised as a Lutheran and am now an Episcopalian, I think the Methodist fourfold understanding of sources of authority for the Christian life is most complete: Scripture, tradition, reason, and experience. Combining these and putting matters very compactly and simply, I see the Christian life as having three central components.

1. *Radical centering in God.*

I see this as the central meaning of "the great commandment" in which Jesus quotes the central affirmation of the Jewish tradition: "Hear, O Israel: the Lord is our God, the Lord is one; and you shall love the Lord your God with all your heart, and with all your soul, and with all your mind, and with all your strength." I also see it as the central meaning of spirituality, which I define as becoming conscious of and intentional about a deepening relationship with God. It leads to that radical centering in God that we see in Jesus as a Jewish mystic and wisdom teacher. As I see Jesus, he knew the immediacy of access to God in his own experience, and as a wisdom teacher he invited his followers into the same kind of immediate relationship to the sacred. This relationship is not only central, it is also transformative.

2. *Compassion and a passion for justice in the world of the everyday.*

I see this as the central meaning of the second half of the great commandment: "You shall love your neighbor as yourself." And in order to express the ethical passion that I see at the center of the biblical tradition, I need both words: compassion and justice. Compassion without justice easily becomes individualized. Justice without compassion easily sounds "only" political. Moreover, the two words are related: justice is the social form of compassion.

Perhaps Dale would agree with me that compassion is the core ethical value for Jesus. But the apocalyptic Jesus provides little basis for seeking justice in this world. He can be seen as indicting the injustices of the world; indeed, that is why the world needs God's apocalyptic intervention. But the apocalyptic Jesus provides no warrant for *seeking to transform* this world; rather, the transformation will occur only through the apocalyptic act of God. On the other hand, my understanding of Jesus as a social prophet and movement initiator points to his passion for God's justice.

3. *Living within a community that celebrates, mediates, and embodies this vision.*

Community is utterly central in the Hebrew Bible and early Christianity. An individualistic spirituality is quite foreign to the biblical vision of life with God. In its worship and practices, the community celebrates life with God, nourishes and mediates the new way of being, and embodies the egalitarian social vision running through the Bible from Exodus through the Jesus movement and evident in early Christianity. Christian life in community is meant to create an alternative world, a counter-world, to the world of normalcy and domination.

It is not essential that this vision of the Christian life be grounded in what we can glimpse of the historical Jesus. All of it is found elsewhere in the Bible. Spirituality, understood as a deepening and faithful relationship with God, is manifestly central to the Bible as a whole. A passion for God's justice in the world can be grounded in Moses and the prophets. It can also be grounded in "reason," for I think that reason untainted by self-interest and class-interest leads to the central realizations that undergird a passion for social justice. So also for the biblical vision of alternative community, which has sources other than Jesus.

Rather, what is at stake is whether Jesus as a figure of history can be claimed for a compelling vision of the Christian life, whether my own or another. The apocalyptic Jesus does not yield a compelling image. We might admire his heroism, the depth of his conviction, and his passion for the wrongs of this world being eventually righted by God. But we would also conclude that the historical Jesus is not only a stranger to our time (as any first-century person would be), but also largely irrelevant to our time.

Of course, the fact that this is at stake should not affect one's historical judgment about what was central to Jesus. And it is hard, so very hard, to know whether it has. Do I see the Jesus I see because I want the Christian life to look like what I want it to look like? Do I see Jesus the way I do because I want following him to look like this? Or have I been led to see the Christian life this way because of what I see in Jesus?

I do not know how I could ever know with any degree of certainty the answer to this question. But my not knowing does not produce paralysis. In part, this is because I see the historical Jesus as consistent with the major voices of the biblical tradition. And for me, the biblical vision is largely unaffected by competing hypotheses about Jesus. Yet it does seem to me that Jesus can be claimed for that vision. Rather than being irrelevant, he strikes me as the crystallization of what is most central in the biblical vision of life. He is, to echo John, the Word and Wisdom of God made flesh. He does not bring a unique revelation, but like the lens in a magnifying glass concentrates the rays of the sun into intense and flaming light.

To conclude, I return to the central meaning of Christianity's christological affirmation: Jesus shows us what a life full of God looks like. In the passion of Jesus, we see the passion of God. By the passion of Jesus, I do not mean his death in particular, though his death was the consequence of his passion. I mean his passionate conviction that God is immediately accessible, and his passion for God's justice in the world of the everyday. To echo a statement from the hasidic stream of Judaism and to refer it to Jesus: Jesus shows us the importance of affirming, for God's sake, both one's self and the world, and by so doing, to transform both.

## JOHN DOMINIC CROSSAN

In this debate I have programmatically declined the simplicity of taking sides for a "non-apocalyptic Jesus" as against an "apocalyptic Jesus." I need descriptions, definitions, and distinctions on both sides to make sure, not that I am on the wrong side of the argument, but that I am not on the right side of the wrong argument. I have insisted that, for then and now, for past and present, we must distinguish between options like destruction or transformation of world, extermination or conversion of enemy, instant or duration of event, passivity or activity of program. I have proposed, for example, that two apocalyptic Christian Jews could agree completely on those eschatological pagans incoming by divine action but also disagree profoundly on any pro-active mission to assist the hand of God. (Stay in Jerusalem, Paul, and pray!). Also, we still have to face the interaction of literal and metaphorical language (and if metaphorical, then metaphorical of what?).

In a passing footnote, Dale mentioned that in his experience "many critical New Testament scholars began life as fundamentalists."[4] That may well be true, but I at least did not, because I grew up in a place and time that had different fundamentalisms among which a biblical one was not even on the horizon. In any case, we must all be very careful about dumping our fundamentalism back into the first century. I myself presume that we are no smarter and no dumber than they were, that we have infinitely more informa-

4. Allison, *Jesus*, 38, note 112.

tion and power but not a whit more wisdom, and that they operated with their religious language on an equal spectrum from 100% literal to 100% metaphorical, stopping at all the way-stations in between. The problem in discerning any given way-station is not just that of temporal or spatial distance but is inherent in the determination itself. We cannot even be sure of one another, here and now. On the one hand, to repeat myself, where now is any given viewer of *The Sixth Sense* on ghosts, or any given reader of the tabloids on wonders, miracles, and prophecies? How would you find out and could you trust the answers one way or another? On the other hand, we are certain that then writers who had just penned ancient pseudepigraphical writings knew what they had done, as, presumably, did those most immediately concerned with their propagation. When, where, and for whom, did that 100% metaphorical evolve into 100% literal?

For this final section, however, I leave all that very much unfinished business to one side. I focus now on just one point because it is, for me, the ultimately most important one, the one where most is at stake for contemporary Christianity. It has to do with the character of Christianity's God. Is that God violent or not?

To survive in the present secular and/or religious culture I find it necessary to make a clear distinction in my mind between disbelief and unconcern. I need to conserve disbelief for vital matters like prejudice, hatred, and discrimination, for anti-semitism, racism, sexism, and homophobia. For many other matters, I prefer unconcern. That includes everything from UFOs and aliens to afterlife and regeneration. Whatever. If apocalyptic eschatology were simply about the imminent "end of the world," I would probably put it in that second category of unconcern and not waste disbelief on something with such a dismally wrong record to date. And if that were all the historical Jesus or earliest Christianity had to proclaim, it would be inexplicable to me how and why it was still around after two millennia of error. Once again, unconcern not disbelief. But even apart from how such an imminent consummation may affect present existence, there is this fundamental question: What is the character of the God presumed behind such an expected event and how at its most profound level does that presumption infect our imaginations? If, for instance, that God's final solution to the problem of evil is the slaughter of the evildoers, why can we not do the same here and now in preparation, participation, or even initiation of apocalyptic consummation? Do we not have the right or even obligation to be the killer children of a Killer God?

What if conversion rather than extermination is emphasized with regard to pagans as evil doers? It seems quite certain that earliest Christianity opted for the conversion rather than extermination strand of its Jewish tradition. James of Jerusalem, for example, would hardly have accepted non-circumcised males and non-koshered members into full participation within the Kingdom movement under any other circumstances. I understand that as the content of the Jerusalem Agreement in Gal 2:1–10. There would be in other words, a mission under Torah-ritual for Jews and a mission without Torah-ritual for gentiles, a two-wing community, as it were. But, for James, if and when two such local communities ate together, kosher regulations were to be observed by all. That is how I understand the Antioch Disagreement in Gal 2:11–14. The only way I can grasp James' position is that the apocalyptic miracle of Gentile conversion (to Jewish monotheism and ethical rules but not to Jewish circumcision and purity rules) was already happening and must be accepted as God's will. If and when one is imagining that consummation, what is the character of a God so imagined? In that scenario, the grand finale was not war but banquet, not a lord of hosts but a host of non-lords.

Here, precisely, is where the contemporary question presses most heavily for me. I take it for granted that we have just finished the most violent century in the history of the world. Maybe others were just as violent by intention but we first obtained the power to do it by execution. Against that background, apocalyptic consummation by final extermination of evildoers puts transcendence squarely within the ambience of evil. It is simply the Biggest Evil around. And, as such it justifies all the lesser evils done in its name. But what about the very idea of the ultimate victory of good over evil however done, even if done by conversion? Is that very idea, and the character of the God thereby imagined, already violent?

I know that question seems immediately absurd. How can you not want and work for the final victory of good over evil? Even if we disagreed on what and where each of those categories existed in concrete cases, how could you disagree on the general hope that good might finally triumph over evil? Do we not need it at least as a horizon that leads us ever onward towards a goal we may never reach but must always attempt? Even if we manage to avoid terms such as "victory" or "triumph," is the very idea of "win," some form of violence all in itself? However you imagine the immanence of transcendence, is it present at best as draw and never, ever as win? An affirmative answer to that question should not result in despair. We have always talked about the final "victory" of good over evil but, on the evidence of that last century, evil is winning hands down. It seems to me that it will take everything we have and more to break even, and to do that effectively, we may have to abandon the delusion that God will some day do it for us, even non-violently.

In summary. After we have made all those distinctions I proposed as necessary to understand what actually happened from John the Baptist through the historical Jesus and on into Paul, the Q Gospel, and Mark, and also after we have drawn contemporary implications from them for the future of Christianity, we are still left with one very fundamental question. Granted that we can struggle non-violently with a violent world only if we are grounded in transcendent non-violence, is the latter committed to a win or a draw; and would we be profoundly wise to negate the former goal as well as unbelievably fortunate to attain the latter one?

## STEPHEN PATTERSON

### Is the Question Pertinent?

Let us assume that critical study of the Bible and Christian origins is of significance to Christians today. Let us also assume that Christian theologians still consider critical biblical interpretation to be one of the foundation stones of critical theological reflection. And let us assume that the historical Jesus – what Jesus actually said and did – is in some way still relevant for Christian faith and practice. These assumptions must all be presumed valid before one can even begin to answer this question. Let me say at the outset, however, that I am skeptical of all of them, even though I believe they all ought to be true. Most Christians are completely unaware of the sort of debate we are having, and many theologians, noting this, have abandoned the field of critical biblical study altogether. So let us assume this question's pertinence, but bear in mind that the preaching of Jesus – whether it was oriented to apocalyptic, wisdom, or to some other alternative – may not be relevant to the way moderns think about their Christian faith at all.

## Apocalyptic and Wisdom: There is a Difference

The historical argument we have been having is not a small one. We are arguing over what sort of religious faith Jesus inspired. To give concrete shape to this debate, I would offer two texts from the New Testament, which perhaps will illustrate the choices involved. The first is Mark 13:24–27:

> But in those days, after the tribulation, the sun will be darkened, and the moon will not give its light, and the stars will be falling from heaven, and the powers in the heavens will be shaken. And then they will see the Son of Man coming in clouds with great power and glory. And then he will send out the angels, and gather his elect from the four winds, from the ends of the earth to the ends of heaven.

This is a classic apocalyptic text. It is preceded by an enumeration of true and false signs, the random violence of the "tribulation," and exhortation to remain faithful to the end. Finally, as the end comes, the elect are gathered in by the Son of man, as the cosmos falls apart in destruction. This concept lies near to the heart of apocalyptically oriented Christianity.

The second text is Luke 17:20–21:

> Being asked by the Pharisees when the kingdom of God was coming, he answered them, "The kingdom of God is not coming with signs to be observed; nor will they say, 'Lo, here it is!' or 'There!' for behold, the kingdom of God is in the midst of you."

This is an anti-apocalyptic text. The basic elements of the apocalyptic worldview are rejected: the ideal time is not future, but present. There are no signs of its coming; it is already here. What shall we call the religious sensibility expressed in these words? The idea that God's rule might be realized in the midst of the human drama, now, is a theme at home in wisdom theology. It is the idea that makes sense of a tradition of parables and aphorisms, which speak of how to live lives responsive to God's wisdom and justice. I will therefore call this sapientially oriented Christianity.

Between these two texts a choice must be made. They are not compatible, even though Luke the evangelist does his best to braid them into a single strand (see 17:22ff.). Luke was not confused. He was just eager to write Christian history into single, unified story – a well-known tendency of this writer. But if Jesus had said both of these things, we would have to assume that he was confused, and that his preaching was not coherent. Is the kingdom already present or does it lie beyond a future, cataclysmic horizon? Are there to be signs of its coming or not?

## Two Different Religions

When one thinks about these two different approaches to the presence of God in human life, one soon discovers that beneath these surface contradictions there lie two very different ways of being religious, perhaps even two different religions.

Let us take the question of epistemology – how God is made known – for starters. In apocalyptic, God is revealed through the esoteric interpretation of signs in scripture or history. Revelation is coded; to receive it one must possess the decoder key. In wisdom, God is revealed through contemplation of the human situation. It is available to anyone willing to look for God in the world; it is not secret or hidden, though it may well go unnoticed.

Or let us take the question of *epiphaneia* – how God is present in the world. In apocalyptic, God is not present, but will come at some future time. God's arrival is marked by violent upheaval and random destruction (note the loss of innocents in Mark 13:14–20). In wisdom, God is already present, though seldom noticed and heeded. God is present in insight and wisdom, and is made known through acts of wisdom, justice and mercy.

Or let us take the question of ethics. In apocalyptic, one observes the commandments of God in fear and trembling of the wrath to come. In wisdom, one seeks after the good, the right thing to do in the midst of life's complexities. Wisdom ethics requires discernment. Apocalyptic ethics requires obedience.

Or finally, let us take the character of God in each – the theology, properly speaking, in each system. In both, God is a just God, empowering the good, thwarting the evil. But in imagining how God achieves that just new world, these traditions represent clear alternatives. In apocalyptic, justice is achieved through violence. The images apocalyptic invokes are frequently martial. The God of apocalyptic is frequently the God of war. In wisdom, justice is achieved through wise living. The images wisdom invokes are frequently educational. The God of wisdom is frequently the God of learning.

These two ways of thinking are not utterly different. They have important things in common. Both counter-cultural wisdom and apocalypticism share the conviction that the world as human beings have constructed and construed it is not God's world of love and justice. They share the idea that God is at work for change. But how do we get to that new reality God holds out? For apocalyptic Christianity the answer was that God would bring it about through violence. For wisdom Christianity the answer was that human beings would bring it about through wise and just living.

The apocalyptic Jesus and the sapiential Jesus are two quite different figures, and they inspire different religions. This is what is at stake for modern Christianity. If Jesus and his preaching still matter to Christian faith today, then the debate we are having is really about what sort of religion Christianity is. What is its claim about God? Is the Christian God the fearsome God of apocalyptic, who brings about justice through violent intervention? Or is the Christian God the one who beckons in the voice of Wisdom, standing on the street corner calling the world passing by to a new commitment to love and justice? Or, as Dom Crossan has so succinctly put it: should we be waiting for God to act, or is God waiting for us to act?

# Bibliography

## Allison, Dale C., Jr.

"The Eschatology of Jesus." In Volume 1. *The Origins of Apocalypticism in Judaism and Christianity.* Ed. John J. Collins. From *The Encyclopedia of Apocalypticism.* Eds. Bernard McGinn, et al. New York: Continuum, 2000. Pp. 267–302

*The Intertextual Jesus: Scripture in Q.* Valley Forge, PA: Trinity Press International, 2000.

*Jesus of Nazareth: Millenarian Prophet.* Minneapolis: Fortress Press, 1998.

*The Jesus Tradition in Q.* Harrisburg, PA: Trinity Press International, 1997.

"A Plea for Thoroughgoing Eschatology." *Journal of Biblical Literature* 113 (1994): 651–68.

## Borg, Marcus

*Conflict, Holiness, and Politics in the Teaching of Jesus.* Lewiston, NY and Queenstown, ON: Edwin Mellen Press, 1984. Rev. ed., Harrisburg, PA: Trinity Press International, 1998.

*Jesus: A New Vision.* San Francisco: HarperSanFrancisco, 1987.

"Jesus and Eschatology: Current Reflections." In *Jesus in Contemporary Scholarship.* Valley Forge, PA: Trinity Press International, 1994. Pp. 69–96.

*The Meaning of Jesus: Two Visions.* With N. T. Wright. San Francisco: HarperSanFrancisco, 1998.

*Meeting Jesus Again for the First Time.* San Francisco: HarperSanFrancisco, 1994.

"A Temperate Case for a Non-Eschatological Jesus." *Forum* 2 (1986): 81–102. Reprinted in *Jesus in Contemporary Scholarship.* Valley Forge, PA: Trinity Press International, 1994. Pp. 47–68.

## Burkett, Delbert

*The Son of Man Debate.* Society for New Testament Studies Monograph Series 107. Cambridge: Cambridge University Press, 1999.

## Collins, John J.

"The Sybilline Oracles." In *Old Testament Pseudepigrapha.* Volume 1. *Apocalyptic Literature and Testaments.* Ed. James H. Charlesworth. Garden City, NY: Doubleday & Company, 1983. Pp. 317–472.

"The Symbolism of Transcendence in Jewish Apocalyptic." In *Papers of the Chicago Society of Biblical Research* 19 (1974): 5–22.

## Conzelmann, Hans

"Present and Future in the Synoptic Tradition." In *God and Christ: Existence and Province.* Journal for Theology and Church 5. Ed Robert W. Funk. New York: Harper & Row, 1968. Pp. 26–44.

## Crossan, John Dominic

*The Birth of Christianity.* San Francisco: HarperSanFrancisco, 1998.

*The Historical Jesus: The Life of a Mediterranean Jewish Peasant.* San Francisco: HarperSanFrancisco, 1991.

*In Parables: The Challenge of the Historical Jesus.* New York: Harper & Row, 1973. Reprinted, Sonoma: Polebridge Press, 1992.

*Jesus: A Revolutionary Biography.* San Francisco: HarperSanFrancisco, 1994.

"Materials and Methods in Historical Jesus Research." *Forum* 4/4 (1988): 3–24.

## Davies, W. D.

"Apocalyptic and Pharisaism." In *Christian Origins and Judaism.* New York: Arno, 1973. Pp. 19–30.

## Dawes, Gregory W. (ed.).

*The Historical Jesus Quest: A Foundational Anthology.* Leiden: Deo Publishing, 1999.

## Dodd, C. H.

*Historical Tradition in the Fourth Gospel.* Cambridge: Cambridge University Press, 1963.

## Fredriksen, Paula

*Jesus of Nazareth, King of the Jews: A Jewish Life and the Emergence of Christianity.* New York: Alfred A. Knopf, 1999.

"Judaism, the Circumcision of Gentiles, and Apocalyptic Hope: Another Look at Galatians 1 and 2." *Journal of Theological Studies* 42 (1991): 532–64.

## Gutiérrez, Gustavo

*The God of Life.* Maryknoll, NY: Orbis Press, 1991.

## Hiers, Richard H.

*Jesus and the Future: Unresolved Questions for Eschatology.* Atlanta: John Knox Press, 1981.

## Jacobson, Arland

*The First Gospel: An Introduction to Q.* Sonoma: Polebridge Press, 1992.

*Wisdom Christology in Q.* Ph.D. Dissertation, Claremont Graduate School, 1978.

## Jülicher, Adolf

*Die Gleichnisreden Jesu*, 2 volumes. Tübingen: J. C. B. Mohr, 1888, 1889.

**Käsemann, Ernst**
"The Beginnings of Christian Theology." In *New Testament Questions for Today*. Philadelphia: Fortress Press, 1969. Pp. 82–107.

**Kloppenborg, John**
*The Formation of Q: Trajectories in Ancient Wisdom Collections*. Philadelphia: Fortress Press, 1987.
"Symbolic Eschatology and the Apocalypticism of Q." *Harvard Theological Review* 80 (1987): 287–306.

**Koch, Klaus**
*The Rediscovery of Apocalyptic*. Naperville, IL: Allenson, 1972.

**Koester, Helmut**
*Ancient Christian Gospels: Their History and Development*. Harrisburg, PA: Trinity Press International, 1990.
"Dialog und Spruchüberlieferung in den gnostichen Texten von Nag Hammadi." *Evangelische Theologie* 39 (1979): 532–56.
"Gnostic Sayings and Controversy Traditions in John 8:12–59." In *Nag Hammadi, Gnosticism, and Early Christianity*. Ed. Charles Hedrick and Robert Hodgson, Jr. Peabody, MA: Hendrickson Publishers, 1986. Pp. 97–110.
"Jesus: The Victim." *Journal of Biblical Literature* 111 (1992): 3–15.
"One Jesus and Four Primitive Gospels." *Harvard Theological Review* 61 (1968): 203–247. Reprinted in *Trajectories Through Early Christianity*. Helmut Koester and James M. Robinson. Philadelphia: Fortress Press, 1971. Pp. 158–204.

**Lapide, Pinchas**
*The Sermon on the Mount*. Maryknoll, NY: Orbis Press, 1986.

**Lindars, Barnabas**
"The Place of the Old Testament in the Formation of New Testament Theology." *New Testament Studies* 23 (1976): 59–66.

**Lührmann, Dieter**
*Die Redaktion der Logienquelle*. Neukirchener-Vluyn: Neukirchener Verlag, 1969.

**Manson, T. W.**
*The Sayings of Jesus*. London: SCM, 1949.

**Miller, Robert J.**
"Is the Apocalyptic Jesus History?" In *The Once and Future Faith*. Ed. Robert W. Funk. Santa Rosa: Polebridge Press, 2001. Pp. 99-114.
*The Jesus Seminar and Its Critics*. Santa Rosa: Polebridge Press, 1999.

## Patterson, Stephen

"The End of Apocalypse: Rethinking the Eschatological Jesus." *Theology Today* 52,1 (1995): 29–48.

*The God of Jesus.* Valley Forge, PA: Trinity Press International, 1998.

Review of Dale C. Allison, *Jesus of Nazareth: Millenarian Prophet. Journal of Biblical Litertaure* 119 (2000): 357–60.

"Wisdom in Q and Thomas." In *In Search of Wisdom: Essays in Honor of John G. Gammie.* Ed. Leo Perdue et al. Louisville: Westminster/John Knox Press, 1993. Pp. 187–221.

## Perrin, Norman

"Wisdom and Apocalyptic in the Message of Jesus." In *Proceedings of the Society of Biblical Literature*, volume 2. Ed. Lane C. McGaughy. Cambridge, MA: Society of Biblical Literature, 1972. Pp. 544–70.

## Ritschl, Albrecht

"Instruction in the Christian Religion." In *Albrecht Ritschl: Three Essays.* Philadelphia: Fortress Press, 1972 (first published 1875).

## Schweitzer, Albert

*The Mystery of the Kingdom of God: The Secret of Jesus' Messiahship and Passion.* London: A & C Black, 1925 (first published 1901).

*The Quest of the Historical Jesus.* New York: Macmillan, 1968 (first published 1906).

## Strobel, August

*Kerygma und Apokalyptik: Ein religionsgeschichtlicher und theologischer Beitrag zur Christusfrage.* Göttingen: Vandenhoeck & Ruprecht, 1967.

## Vielhauer, Philipp

"Gottesreich und Menschensohn in der Verkündigung Jesu." In *Festschrift für Günther Dehn.* Ed. W. Schneemelcher. Neukirchen: Buchhandlung des Erziehungsvereins, 1957. Pp. 51–79.

## Weiss, Johannes

*Jesus' Proclamation of the Kindgom of God.* Philadelphia: Fortress Press, 1971 (first published 1892).

## Wilder, Amos

*Eschatology and Ethics in the Teaching of Jesus.* New York: Harper & Brothers, 1939.

## Wright, Nicholas Thomas

*Jesus and the Victory of God*, vol.2 of *Christian Origins and the Question of God.* Minneapolis: Fortress Press, 1997.